Liberal Union of Ireland

An Examination of the Home Rule Bill of 1893.

With an Appendix Containing the Full Text of the Measure Itself

Liberal Union of Ireland

An Examination of the Home Rule Bill of 1893.
With an Appendix Containing the Full Text of the Measure Itself

ISBN/EAN: 9783337169886

Printed in Europe, USA, Canada, Australia, Japan

Cover: Foto ©Suzi / pixelio.de

More available books at **www.hansebooks.com**

OF THE

HOME RULE BILL OF 1893.

𝔚ith an 𝔄ppendix

CONTAINING

THE FULL TEXT OF THE MEASURE ITSELF.

DUBLIN:

HODGES, FIGGIS, & CO. (LTD.), 104, GRAFTON-STREET.
WILLIAM M'GEE, 18, NASSAU-STREET.

PUBLISHED BY

THE LIBERAL UNION OF IRELAND, 45, DAME-ST., DUBLIN.

APRIL, 1893.

PREFACE.

In publishing the following Report on the provisions of the Government of Ireland Bill, the Executive Council of the Liberal Union of Ireland think it well, by way of preface, to republish the following resolution, adopted soon after the introduction of the Bill:—

"That, having considered the Government of Ireland Bill, 1893, the Liberal Union of Ireland is as strongly as ever convinced that no system of separate Legislature can be devised which will not be fraught with injury and disaster to Ireland and to Great Britain; that the measure, as introduced by Mr. Gladstone, places Ireland in a position of permanent inferiority to Great Britain, and would, if passed, be destructive of the best interests of the country, and would tend to perpetuate disunion and strife both in Ireland and between Ireland and Great Britain, and that no amendment of the Bill can render its essential principle just, or its operation beneficial."

The more full and careful consideration, which the Executive Council have since given to the details of the Bill has confirmed them in the opinion expressed in this resolution.

They are strengthened in their conviction that the establishment of a separate Legislature in Ireland, with an Executive dependent on it, must end in disaster. The Bill proposes a system of financial relations between Ireland and the Imperial Government, which at the outset must create a conflict of interests sure to engender animosity and strife,—whilst, so far as the internal affairs of Ireland are concerned, her new Government is treated with such distrust, and so rigidly bound in financial fetters as to be foredoomed to failure. This much-vaunted message of peace must prove the starting-point of a new and embittered struggle.

That Mr. Gladstone, with his long Parliamentary practice, and the experience gained by his failure in 1886, should now, after seven years of study and preparation, produce a measure so absolutely unworkable and mischievous, is a clear proof that the Home Rule problem is incapable of solution, in the practical form of an Act of Parliament. Immense injury has already been caused to the whole United Kingdom by the mere introduction, on Ministerial responsibility, of this proposal, as an alternative to the continuous and steady administration of Irish affairs under the existing Constitution by an Executive directly responsible to the Imperial Parliament—a Parliament which has shown itself both able and willing to grant to Ireland redress of every real grievance, and to carry into effect every legislative change proved to be requisite or desirable in her interest.

The more closely the Bill is looked at, the more dangerous will its concessions appear, and the more illusory its safeguards. As a contribution to an exact and dispassionate examination of the Bill the present pamphlet has been prepared.

THE GOVERNMENT OF IRELAND BILL,

1893.

THE Bill " to amend the provision for the Government of Ireland," which was introduced into the House of Com- mons, on the 13th of February last, by Mr. Gladstone, is, in its framework, the same Bill that was rejected on its second reading in 1886. There have been many changes made in the draft, some merely verbal, others small and unimportant, and several large and most material ; but on the whole the Bill of 1893 is the Bill of 1886, with certain alterations put in for the purpose of meeting objections coming from friends rather than from foes.   In the first place, the principle underlying both Bills is the same ; they both purport to hand over all the powers which are naturally vested in an indepen- dent Legislature, to the Statutory Legislature of Ireland, save such as are therein afterwards excepted.   The second clause in the Bill of 1893, though it differs slightly in language from the corresponding section of the Bill of 1886, has pre- cisely the same meaning.   It will be sufficient to quote the clause in the Bill of 1893.

" With the exceptions and subject to the restrictions in this Act mentioned, there shall be granted to the Irish Legislature power to make laws for the peace, order, and good government of Ireland in respect of matters exclusively relating to Ireland or some part thereof."

In other words, subject to the exceptions which appear on the face of the Bill, sovereign power is handed over to the Irish Legislature.

B

This, in itself, is somewhat startling. A supreme Parliament, desiring to keep itself supreme, would be much more likely to delegate certain definite rights and duties to a subordinate assembly, keeping within itself the great mass of undefined and almost indefinable powers, than to divest itself of all these powers, with certain specific exceptions and restrictions. The case of Ireland is so different from anything to be found elsewhere throughout the world, that there are very few analogies which afford much help. In the United States and in Germany, where a federal system is in existence, the various " States " delegated powers to the central government to be used in a certain manner and for certain specific purposes, but the Legislatures which were sovereign before, remained sovereign still, save with regard to those matters over which they had renounced their control. In Canada, on the other hand, definite powers were delegated by the Dominion Parliament to the subordinate legislatures, and the sovereignty remained in the supreme and central government. Mr. Gladstone, curiously enough, has gone for his pattern not to the most analogous case, namely, that of Canada, but rather to cases absolutely distinct in principle and standing on a different basis. The federal idea runs all through his arrangement, and yet federation cannot enter into his calculation, and is under the circumstances impossible. Ireland is, with important exceptions, given the powers which a sovereign State, desirous, for the purposes of defence or otherwise, of coming together with one or more other sovereign States, would reserve to itself.

To this it may be answered that the Imperial Parliament is still supreme, and that the Bill recites in its preamble the fact of this supremacy.

Federal systems—United States, Germany, Canada.

Supremacy of Imperial Parliament.

" Whereas it is expedient that without impairing or restricting the supreme authority of Parliament, an Irish Legislature should be created for such purposes in Ireland as in this Act mentioned.''

The words of a preamble to a Bill have no legal force whatever, except so far as they throw light on the meaning of some clause in the Bill itself. As a matter of fact, these words do throw light on a clause at the very end of the Bill, which is of enormous importance. Clause 33 enacts that:

"The Irish Legislature may repeal or alter any provision of this Act which is by this Act expressly made alterable by that Legislature, and also any enactments in force in Ireland, except such as either relate to matters beyond the powers of the Irish Legislature, *or being enacted by Parliament after the passing of this Act may be expressly extended to Ireland.* An Irish Act, notwithstanding it is in any respect repugnant to any enactment excepted as aforesaid, shall, though read subject to that enactment, be, except to the extent of that repugnancy, valid.''

The words in italics give power to the Imperial Parliament at any time to pass an Act relating to Ireland, which the Irish Legislature may not repeal or alter.

The Bill, therefore, first asserts the absolute sovereignty of the Imperial Legislature, then makes another Legislature sovereign, save as to certain definite subjects, and finally proceeds to give the Parliament in Westminster power to legislate over the head of the sovereign Legislature which it has created. The result could not but be disastrous. A conflict of powers and of claims must arise which a court might decide, but could never really settle.

It is impossible to find any word which will express the position of such a Legislature. It is not "co-ordinate" with the Imperial Legislature, for Acts of Parliament can be passed by the latter dealing with matters under the jurisdiction of the Irish Legislature without its consent ; and it is not truly subordinate, for it is quasi-sovereign.

It is not difficult to imagine circumstances arising under which the Imperial Legislature might be almost forced to pass some Act having Ireland within its scope. This Act would, in all probability, be one which the Irish Legislature could, but would not pass. Immediately a conflict must arise, and the Legislature in Dublin would say : " You have given us complete powers of legislation in this particular matter. How, then, can you also legislate with regard to it ? Either our power is complete, or it is not. If it is, then you are acting *ultra vires;* if it is not, then the second section of the Act is a nullity—a mere paper right—a power *de jure,* and not *de facto.*" It is clear that such a fundamental dispute as this could only end by the Imperial Legislature either conceding everything, or destroying the statutory Parliament: in other words, reconquering the country.

EXCEPTIONS FROM THE POWERS OF THE IRISH LEGISLATURE.

Restrictions. It follows from the above, that whether the Irish Legislature be sovereign or not, it will probably act as if sovereign, subject, of course, to the exceptions and restrictions set forth in clauses 3 and 4. Clauses 3 is tolerably clear.

Crown. " The Irish Legislature shall not have power to make laws in in respect to—(1) the Crown, or the succession to the Crown, or the Regency, or the Lord Lieutenant as representative of the War. Crown ; (2) the making of peace or war, or matters arising from a state of war ; "

It could not, for instance, declare itself neutral, or legislate as to prize or booty of war ; but it might pass resolutions expressing sympathy with one of the combatants in a European war, and by so doing might bring the Queen's Government into great trouble. For instance, if an Irish Legislature had existed in 1870, the probability is that it would have passed many resolutions of sympathy with France. Such resolutions would have been immediately followed by peremptory demands for explanation from Prince Bismarck.

Naval or military forces. " (3) Naval or military forces or the defence of the realm ; "

It could not, for instance, meddle with the coastguards. In the Bill of 1886 the words *militia and volunteers* were inserted in this 3rd sub-clause. It is clear that militia would come under the words military forces ; but a very serious question might arise as to whether the sub-clause would prevent the Irish Legislature from equipping and subsidizing a volunteer force.

"(4) Treaties with foreign States; (5) dignities or titles of honour; (6) Treason, treason-felony, alienage and naturalization; (7) trade with any place out of Ireland, quarantine and navigation; (8) beacons, lighthouses, &c.; (9) coinage, legal tender, standard of weights and measures; (10) trade marks, copyright or patent rights." Treaties, &c.

Most of these are matters which in any federal system would of necessity be left to the federal Government; and even if the Irish Legislature had the sovereign powers to which it will probably lay claim, it would not be likely to quarrel about them. The seventh restriction, however, is one which it is certain to endeavour, by fair means or foul, to get repealed. The one thing, which Irishmen of nearly all shades of opinion believe in, is protection for Irish industries. Sub-clause 7 prevents the Legislature from putting on any kind of duty, or, indeed, meddling in any way with the imports into Ireland. Neither will it be able to give direct bounties to Irish manufacturers, for the purpose of encouraging an export trade. It might, however, indirectly do the same thing by, for instance, relieving certain kinds of manufactures from local taxation, or by otherwise assisting particular industries. Trade.

FURTHER RESTRICTIONS.

Clause 4 says, that

"The power of the Irish Legislature shall not extend to the making of any law: (1) respecting the establishment or endowment of religion or prohibiting the free exercise thereof; (2) imposing any disability or conferring any privilege on account of religious belief;" Establishment and endowment of religion. Religious privileges.

There is, however, nothing to prevent large grants being made to convent schools in aid of education, or even to individual bishops or priests for the same purpose, or, for that matter, for the purpose of building churches and cathedrals, or, indeed, for almost any other exclusively religious purpose; nor is there anything to prevent the Irish Legislature permitting religious processions through the streets, or passing an Act making words spoken in contempt of the Catholic Church, or even of a priest, sacrilege, and a crime entailing severe punishment.

Denominational Charity. "(3) The abrogating or prejudicially affecting the right to establish or maintain any place of denominational education or any denominational institution or charity;"

This sub-clause will not prevent the Legislature from specially taxing such institutions, or from appointing inspectors for the purpose of spying on and harassing the inmates, or of punishing the governors and managers severely, in cases of supposed proselytism.

Schools. " (4) Prejudicially affecting the right of any child to attend a school receiving public money without attending the religious instruction at that school;"

This will not prevent the Government from handing the schools into the hands of the priests; from allowing them to choose the school books, fix the curriculum, put up religious emblems, and generally to turn the National Schools into denominational institutions. Nor will it prevent the Legislature from refusing grants of public money to any school which does not conform to the standard.

Personal liberty. " (5) Whereby any person may be deprived of life, liberty, or property *without due process of law,* or may be denied the equal protection of the laws, or whereby private property may be taken without just compensation ; or

Corporations. (6) Whereby any existing corporation incorporated by Royal Charter or by any local or general Act of Parliament (not being a corporation raising for public purposes taxes, rates, cess, dues, or tolls, or administering funds so raised) may, unless it consents, *or the leave of Her Majesty is first obtained on address from the two Houses of the Irish Legislature,* be deprived of its rights, privileges, or property *without due process of law ;*"

These two sub-clauses are probably the most illusory in the whole Act. The words "*without due process of law*" are vague and exceedingly elastic; they evidently refer to the executive and judicial processes of the law, and as they are not confined to the present law, they must mean due process of the law existing at the time. When it is recollected what enormous powers the Legislature will have *of changing the law*, it will easily be seen how completely *life, liberty, and property* will be in the hands of those in power. Even without these words it would probably be easy to evade the clause, but with them they become worthless. Sub-clause 6 also gives power to deprive Trinity College, for instance, of its rights, privileges, and property, by leave of Her Majesty on address of the two Houses of the Irish Legislature. Now, it seems likely, considering that the Members of the two Houses would for a long time be the nominees of the clerical party that Her Majesty's Lord Lieutenant would very soon be addressed on the subject, and if he refused more than once or twice to give his assent, there would probably be unpleasant work. {Trinity College.}

" (7) Whereby any inhabitant of the United Kingdom may be deprived of legal rights as respects public sea fisheries." {Sea fisheries.}

This sub-clause is evidently put in to prevent the Irish Legislature from interfering with English, Scotch, and Manx fishing-boats whilst fishing off the Irish coast, but it will not prevent it from practically forbidding them to enter Irish harbours, either by levying excessive port dues, or otherwise.

The above slight criticism of these restrictive sections will show how very illusory any such restrictions are, where virtual sovereignty resides in the restricted Legislature. Detailed as they are in the 3rd and 4th clauses of the Bill, it appears as if an enormous number of matters were excepted from the purview of the Irish Legislature, but if the powers given by the Bill were to be set out side by side with the restrictions, the latter would very quickly shrink to their proper insignificance, and it would be shown how totally inadequate they would be to afford any protection to the minority. For instance, the Irish Legislature would be able to revolutionize the criminal law; might abolish trial by jury; might change the whole system of legal procedure; might relieve clerics from responsibility to the ordinary law of the land, and re-introduce {Powers of the Legislature.}

ecclesiastical courts, before which alone priests could be tried; might legalize the Plan of Campaign by staying all processes for the resumption of possession of land; might take away the right of public meeting; might, in fact alter almost every principle of law, and repeal every Act, by virtue of which, although we think so little about it, our lives, liberties, rights, and properties are now secured, and our social relationships settled.

THE EXECUTIVE (Clause 5).

Executive.

Clause 5 deals with the executive government of Ireland.

The Lord Lieutenant, as representing the Queen, is to be head of the Executive. He is to be aided and advised by an Executive Committee of the Privy Council, " being of such numbers and comprising persons holding such offices as Her Majesty may think fit, *or as may be directed by Irish Act.*"

Executive Committee of Privy Council.

That is to say, the Irish Legislature may direct that the Executive Committee is to be of the number of, say, nine persons, and shall always comprise :—The Prime Minister, the Chancellor of the Exchequer, the Home Secretary, the Lord Chancellor, the Lord Mayor of Dublin, and also such one of the Roman Catholic Bishops for the time being, as shall be Minister for Education; and, apparently, whether they had been called by the Queen to Her Privy Council or not. The clause goes on to provide that, *on the advice of this Executive Committee,* the Lord Lieutenant *shall* give or withhold his assent to Bills which have passed the two Houses of the Irish Legislature, unless special instructions are sent by the Queen in respect of any such Bills.

Cabinet.

It is well to recollect that *the Executive Committee of the Privy Council* is only the legal name for "*the Cabinet.*" The " *Cabinet*" of the United Kingdom, so well known to every politician, is a body unknown to the Law. It is merely a Committee of the Privy Council formed of the great executive officers of State. The Irish Cabinet will thus be the Irish Executive, and will be dependent on popular favour and subject to popular control. This system works well in England, because it has developed slowly through centuries, and is the outcome of the peculiar political genius of Englishmen. In the United States it does not exist. There the Executive is separate from and independent of the Legislature, and is therefore not directly controlled by popular vote. In Ireland, where political passion runs so high, it is a dangerous thing to make the Executive dependent on popular favour. Will Irish ministers, to whom large powers are suddenly granted, have the courage to defy popular demands and to carry out the law justly and firmly? Judging from the men who are likely to be the first Irish ministers, it seems hardly likely, and yet if they do not, revolution will occur in Ireland with all its attendant horrors and confusion. It may further be added that by this Bill the United Kingdom will give up all executive control in Ireland. Not a single executive office will be responsible to the Imperial Parliament, and in case Ireland should refuse to carry out a law made in Westminster, Great Britain will have to employ the army to enforce obedience. There will be no other means left.

THE LEGISLATURE (Clauses 6 & 7).

The clauses dealing with the Constitution of the Irish Legislature are the simplest in the Bill. There are to be two houses, called respectively, the *Irish Legislative Council* and the *Irish Legislative Assembly.* The Council is to consist of 48 Councillors; the Legislative Assembly of 103 members. No man will be entitled to be registered as an elector to vote at the election of Councillor, unless *he owns or occupies land or tenements in the constituency of a rateable value of more than twenty pounds;* the franchise for the Assembly will remain for *six years* the same as at present. The term of office of every Councillor will be *eight years*—will not be affected by a dissolution of the Assembly—and one-half of the Councillors must retire every four years; the Legislative Assembly will, unless sooner dissolved, have continuance for *five years*, and no longer. No elector will be entitled to

(marginal notes:) The Legislature. Legislative Council. Legislative Assembly.

vote *in more than one constituency for a Councillor;* but for the Assembly, the present law will obtain until changed. After

Power to alter Election Laws.

Constitution of the Assembly and Council.

six years from the passing of the Act, the Irish Legislature will be able to alter the qualifications" of electors for the Assembly, the constituencies, and the distribution of members among the constituencies ; but no power is given by clause 6 to alter the election laws dealing with the Council. (Power, however, is given to the Irish Legislature, by clause 32, as explained by the definition ‚of "election laws" given in clause 39, to alter these laws at its pleasure, save such as refer to the qualification of electors.) The constituencies of the Legislative Council are set out in the 1st schedule to the Act; the constituencies to elect the Assembly will remain the same as at present.

The effect of the above clause may be put in a few words. The *Legislative Assembly,* which will be the Irish House of Commons, will for six years number 103 (the number of members now sent to Westminster); will be elected by the same constituencies as these 103, and on the same franchise. After the lapse of six years the Irish Government will be able to introduce "universal suffrage," to double or halve the number of members, to redistribute the representation as they think fit or in any other way to change the present "election laws." The present distribution of seats is extremely unfair. The south and west are greatly over-represented and the north much under-represented. The Bill does not propose to remedy these anomalies, but on the contrary, notwithstanding the principle laid down in clause 7, sub-clause 3, that due regard is to be had to the population in any fresh distribution of the constituencies, it attempts to perpetuate them in the interests of the Nationalists. The *Legislative Council* will correspond in a feeble way to the House of Lords. It will be chosen by an electorate composed of all those who possess lands or houses of the value of £20 and upwards, and no power is given to the Irish Legislature to reduce the franchise. The constituencies, as set out in the schedule, which are to elect this Council have been thoroughly gerrymandered in favour of the majority.

For instance there will be no divisions in large counties or boroughs. Dublin county will not be divided into north and south Dublin, each returning a member, but the whole county will return three members. It is easy to see how this arrangement will prejudice the minority.

Clause 8 provides for the case of a disagreement between the two houses. Under such circumstances, if, after a dissolution, or the lapse of two years from the disagreement, the Bill is again passed by the Legislative Assembly, and fails within three months to be adopted by the Council, the two houses will be bound to meet, deliberate, and vote together on the Bill, and if there is then even a bare majority in its favour it must be sent up to the Lord Lieutenant for his assent or rejection. Now, whatever safeguard for the minority in Ireland is provided by the creation of the second chamber, and it is not much, this clause will entirely destroy such safeguard. Supposing, for the sake of argument, that every member of the Council belonged to the minority, and that they had 23 representatives in the Lower House,—and they could not have more under the present arrangement,—yet they would be outvoted, when the two Houses came together. Forty-eight and twenty-three make seventy-one, and there would be a majority of eighty against them. But the minority could not hope, at the outside, to return anything like one-half of the Councillors, and thus we see that whatever safeguard the existence of the Council might afford is taken away by this clause. It becomes absolutely void and worthless.

Case of disagreement between the two Houses.

REPRESENTATION IN THE HOUSE OF COMMONS.

Clause 9 provides that Ireland shall return eighty members to the House of Commons, and the second schedule to the Act sets out the constituencies which shall elect them. This schedule is just as unfair to the minority as the schedule dealing with the election of Councillors. The counties are *not* divided, but the electors in each will vote as a whole for two, three, or four members, as the case may be ; Ulster is not given its legitimate number ; the southern portions of Ireland are

Eighty Members in the House of Commons.

Dublin University.

Bills dealing with Ireland.

over-represented, and Dublin University is disfranchised. Irish representatives will not be permitted to vote on Bills or motions confined to Great Britain ; but if any English member moves as an amendment that the Bill be extended to Ireland, the Irish members will at once be able to speak and vote on it. It can easily be seen what trouble this will give rise to. At any moment, some Bill, which is Imperial in its scope, may come on in some of its various stages, or some English obstructive may move that the Bill be extended to Ireland. At once the Irish members, who between times are expected to hang about the lobbies of the Houses of Parliament, will be called in, and perhaps a Bill which the Ministry hope to carry, or, as the case may be, to defeat, is thrown out or carried. The amount of confusion which must follow is incalculable, and will make the position of the Ministry, and the orderly carrying on of business, impossible. Besides all this, the difficulty of deciding what is Imperial and what is not will be tremendous. Almost all grants of money might be held to be Imperial. Would, for instance, a grant for the payment of a Labour Commission for England, or of a Commission on Railway Rates, or a grant to the National Gallery to buy some celebrated picture, be votes in which the Irish members might take part ? If so, such votes might be thrown out against the wishes of Englishmen and Scotchmen. Innumerable and fierce disputes must arise over such points, and the Speaker would be suddenly elevated into a *Supreme Court* for the decision of large constitutional questions. Such a condition of things would be intolerable. Even if votes of the above kind did not come within the words of the 3rd schedule, which sets out what is Imperial expenditure, yet the Irish representatives would feel, if they were not allowed to take part, that they were being defrauded of their rights, for Irishmen, undoubtedly, would still contribute to this expenditure. A vote dealing with the *Privy Council*, or the *Meteorological Society*, or *the Civil Service*, which are all set down as Imperial under the schedule, would not be one whit more Imperial *than a grant to the National Gallery*, or the *British Museum*, or a *Commission on Labour*. The schedule

of Imperial expenditure is, in itself, ridiculous. It should Schedule of
either contain a great many more items, or a great many less, Imperial Finance.
and in the latter case Ireland's quota should be much smaller.
It is drawn up on no valid principle whatever.

FINANCE.

The 10th to the 19th clauses of the Bill, both inclusive,
deal with the financial relations between the two countries.
They are by far the most difficult and complicated clauses
of this complicated measure, and the most ruinous to Ireland
—the poorer partner. They separate the finances of the two
countries, and create a distinct Exchequer in Ireland. Into Irish
this Exchequer will be paid all the present Irish Revenue, Exchequer.
with the exception of the *Customs.* The *Customs Duties,* Customs
which amount to almost two millions and a-half, will Duties.
still be regulated, collected, managed, and paid into the
Exchequer of the United Kingdom, as heretofore : that is to
say, English officials will be appointed in every seaport town
in Ireland, and the Irish Legislature will not be allowed to
meddle in any way with them or their functions. The total
Revenue of Ireland is under eight millions and a-half ; and
the Exchequer of the United Kingdom, will, therefore,
receive from the Customs considerably over one quarter as
Ireland's share in Imperial revenue. More than this, the
Customs' duties in Ireland have been, for years past, steadily
growing year by year. If, therefore, the sum fixed now as
properly representing the Imperial liabilities is a fair one,
then Ireland will, on the assumption that the Customs will
increase in the same ratio as heretofore, be paying in ten
years far more than her share, whilst she is getting no return
for her increasing trade.

All other taxes, namely, *excise, income-tax, probate, and* Other Taxes.
*stamp duties, the revenues of the Crown in Ireland, Postal
revenues, licence duties, and all miscellaneous duties,* will be
paid into the Irish Exchequer. All these heads of revenue,
it is calculated, amount together to £5,660,000, while the
expenditure, on the present scale, amounts to £5,160,000.

18   *The Government of Ireland Bill*, 1893.

Surplus to commence business.

The surplus, therefore, which the Irish Legislature will have to commence business on will only be £500,000. When the expenses necessary for the starting of a new Government are considered, this sum will at once be seen to be ridiculously inadequate. A very large portion of this amount, if not the whole, would be necessary in order to take over the Bank of Ireland, and remodel it into a House fit for the Legislature. Ireland would, therefore, probably have to commence her new national life by putting on fresh taxes in order to meet the additional expenditure

First charges on the Irish Exchequer.

necessary. But greater difficulties would arise. There are a large number of charges which must be paid over to the Exchequer of the United Kingdom before a penny can be touched for Irish purposes, namely—(1) sums due for interest and sinking fund payments under the Board of Works, and under former Land Purchase Acts (Lord Ashbourne's) and other loans; (2) money now due under Mr. Balfour's Purchase of Land Act of 1891; (3) salaries, gratuities, and pensions due to *Civil Servants*, which are to be paid in the first instance and for three years, out of the English Exchequer; (4) moneys which may in the future become due under the Purchase Act, and which the Land Purchase accounts may be found insufficient to pay; (5) an annual sum of £5000 for the Lord Lieutenant's Household; (6) all existing charges on the Consolidated Fund, such as for instance the salaries of the Judges, and other such charges. All these must be paid on the certificate of the Controller-General of the United Kingdom by order of the Lord Lieutenant, without any counter-signature, *before any other payment can be made out of the Irish Exchequer for any purpose whatever.* So runs clause 14 of the Bill. Now suppose, an eventuality not at all improbable, that at first the Irish Government found great difficulty in collecting in the interest on the money advanced to tenant farmers for the purchase of their holdings (now nearly ten millions), almost the whole of the available surplus of £500,000 would

Taxation.

disappear, and new taxation would have to be imposed to meet the deficiency. But how could the Irish Government raise the money, or whom could they tax? They could not raise the Excise duties, for they are reserved for the Imperial Parliament to raise or diminish at its pleasure. They might tax the large landowners; but very little could be got out of them, for rents will assuredly not be paid. They could, if they wished, and probably finally would have to tax the land and the tenants, including the new purchasers under Lord Ashbourne's Acts, and under Mr. Balfour's Purchase of Land Act of 1891; but they would hardly be likely to do this, in the first instance, for in so doing they would alienate the great mass of their supporters. It would only remain for them to tax the merchants and professional classes in the towns, and the only manner in which, under such circumstances, they could raise a sufficient sum of money would be by putting on a graduated income tax. Graduated But immediately an attempt was made to levy such a tax, a Income Tax. fresh difficulty would occur. A very large number of mercantile firms have business houses, and business transactions, both in Great Britain and in Ireland, and the income tax is now paid on the profits of the business as a whole and without any attempt being made to separate the profits. Under the Home Rule Bill, even if the tax remained the same in both countries, serious trouble would probably arise between the two Exchequers, over the precise amounts to be paid into each. But immediately the tax was raised in Effect of Ireland all those firms which had offices on both sides of raising the the channel would transfer the management of their business Income Tax. to the less taxed country, converting their houses in Belfast or Dublin into mere agents' offices. Under such circumstances, where would the business be "carried on"? Who would get the tax? The profits would be shown in England on the gross turnover of goods, though sent for actual sale to agents in Ireland. Most certainly the tax would have to be paid, if not altogether, to a very large extent, into the Exchequer of the United Kingdom, and Ireland would consequently suffer.

The very same difficulties and confusion would arise over the collection of the "death duties."

Clause 11, sub-clause 2, seems specially drawn for the purpose of enabling Great Britain to benefit by the frightening of capital out of Ireland and by the transfer of Irish business to head-quarters in England.

"A person shall not be required to pay income-tax in Great Britain in respect of property situate or business carried on in Ireland, *and a person shall not be required to pay income-tax in Ireland in respect of property situate or business carried on in Great Britain.*"

Mercantile Firms.

In view of this clause and of the fear of the tax being raised in Ireland, many persons would certainly endeavour to transfer either their capital or their business to the other side of the channel. It is but fair to add that sub-clause 3 provides for the payment by the Exchequer of the United Kingdom of the difference between the amount collected in Great Britain from British, colonial, and foreign securities held by residents in Ireland, and the amount collected in Ireland from Irish securities held by residents in Great Britain, but it is not suggested how these different amounts are to be arrived at, and, as a matter of fact, they cannot be discovered by any known statistical process. This sub-clause does not affect mercantile firms, nor touch at all the important question of where the business is, in point of law, really carried on; besides which sub-clause 4 will prevent the Irish Government benefiting, as far as the difference to be paid by Great Britain is concerned, for it provides that in calculating such difference the excess of the rate of income-tax in Ireland over the rate in Great Britain is not to be taken into account. In other words, no matter what additional income-tax the Irish Government may put on, it will not affect such income as may be derived from non-Irish securities.

All these clauses dealing with income-tax are exceedingly hard on Ireland. As far as her money matters are concerned Ireland will be " cabined, cribbed, and confined," and in such a way that if she struggles to get out of her shackles, Great Britain will be sure to reap the advantage. An Irish Legislature may raise the income-tax; but, in the first place, it will probably bring in little extra money, and in the second, the tax will only fall on residents in Ireland, holding Irish property or securities, or who are in commercial affairs in the country, whilst those who hold securities out of Ireland will pay at the old rate. Could a neater way be invented of discouraging Irish enterprise?

EXCISE.

The 10th clause allows the Irish Legislature to manage Excise. and collect the Excise on articles consumed in Ireland, but does not allow it to change the amount of the tax itself. The Excise duties will form almost three-fifths of the whole income of Ireland in the future, and consequently it will be of enormous importance to the Government to foster and aid the manufacture and sale of Irish whiskey as far as possible· No matter how the members of the Legislature may desire it, Temperance they will not dare to discourage drinking, by temperance legis- Legislation impossible. lation. Ireland's very existence will depend on the keeping up of the Excise revenue, and her legislators will know that. They will be bound, tied hand and foot, to the liquor interest.

The Bill even prevents an attempt being made to raise Tobacco. an income by the growth and taxing of tobacco beyond what is now permitted, for ALL PROHIBITIONS in connexion with the duties of Excise are kept in the hands of the Imperial Parliament.

Sub-clause 3 of clause 10 is openly and glaringly unfair Articles made to Ireland, for it provides that the Excise duties on articles in Ireland and consumed in made in Ireland, but consumed in Great Britain, shall be Great Britain. paid to the Imperial Exchequer, while there is no counter-balancing clause, giving the duties on articles made in Great Britain and consumed in Ireland to the Irish Exchequer. Ireland will not receive a penny piece on the immense export of whiskey and stout to England and Scotland, nor will she, on the other hand, be allowed to tax English beer or Scotch whiskey imported to her shores. Great Britain, the richer country, will practically receive both differences.

Now, how the Government of Great Britain will be able to Smuggling. prevent a large amount of what will be analogous to smuggling

c

it is hard to understand.   How will they be able to prevent
a large quantity of whiskey being brought across the channel
as passengers' luggage, or packed with duty-free goods,
without erecting Custom houses for the examination of such
luggage ?   If they do not, the revenue of the United
Kingdom will be largely defrauded.   If they do, they can not,
with any justification, prevent Ireland from erecting similar
Custom houses against Great Britain.   Taking Excise duty on
whiskey and stout manufactured in Ireland is in reality pre-
cisely the same thing as putting a Customs' duty against the
Irish product.   Great Britain will be able, immediately the
Bill becomes law, to reduce the Excise on Scotch and English
whiskey and beer, and thus to irreparably injure the Irish
trade, while if a Bill to effect this were introduced into the
House of Commons the Irish members would not be allowed
to speak or vote on it.

Effect of Increase of Excise duty to Ireland.   Again, and in another manner, the Imperial Exchequer
takes care of itself.   Suppose, for instance, a war occurs, or for
some other reason the British Government want an increase
of revenue, and is of opinion that spirits will bear an
additional 2*s.* per gallon.   The Excise duty is accordingly
increased to that extent.   Under sub-clause 5 of clause 10
every penny brought in by this extra 2*s.* must be paid over
to the Imperial Exchequer, even though the effect of the increased duty should be to make the Irish revenue fall off instead of to increase it.   On the other hand; sub-clause 6 provides that if the rates are decreased the United Kingdom shall
not pay to Ireland the amount of the decrease of the rate per
gallon, but only the amount of the deficiency in the revenue
Effect of decrease.   occasioned thereby.   How this deficiency is to be ascertained
the Act does not specify.   Whether it is to be the deficiency,
comparing it with the year immediately preceding, or the
deficiency as compared with the first year of existence of the
Irish Legislature, we are left completely in the dark.   It
really, however, hardly matters.   The whole arrangement
is so very unfair and one-sided, that no body of men, of even
average intellect, could accept it without a secret determination to make short work of it on the first opportunity.

LOCAL LOANS.

At the present moment Ireland owes the Imperial Ex- Local Loans. chequer a matter of over sixteen millions for loans made through the Board of Works and the Land Commission. In 1892 alone a sum of almost £1,000,000 was advanced to various local boards, as well as to farmers large and small, tenants and landlords. After the appointed day no more money for loans will be advanced to Ireland, either by the Commissioners of Public Works or by the Local Loans Fund (see clause 16, sub-clause 3). If a farmer wants money for the purpose of drainage or other land improvement, or a fisherman for buying nets or building boats; if a Harbour Board wants to build docks, or a Public Company wants to erect buildings, and cannot find the money to do so, they will have to go to the Irish Government for help. The Irish Government will not have the money to lend; that is certain. It will have to borrow it somewhere, and as almost all the property of the Government will under the Bill be mortgaged to the United Kingdom to pay all charges due and to become due to the Imperial Exchequer, its credit, if it has any at all, is not likely to stand very high, and it will have to borrow on high terms. When the farmer at last gets his loan, he will have to pay, not 3 per cent. or 3½ per cent. interest, as now, but probably 5 per cent. or 6 per cent. even without any sinking fund arrangement. Clause 16, sub-clause 2, also provides that the Irish Government shall pay off the present amount of the loan (sixteen millions) and the interest thereon, by annuities, paid half-yearly for 49 years, at 4 per cent. on the principal of the loan. This will amount to about £640,000 a-year, and will have to come out of the Income of the Exchequer. Now, suppose the Government have difficulty in collecting in the outstanding loans and interest, how are they to pay their annual charge? It is but fair they should pay it; but the difficulty is, what are they to pay it out of? If they do not pay it, all loans for any purposes will cease, for the very small credit the Government before had will be utterly gone.

LOCAL RATES.

Grants in aid of Local Rates.

There is, however, a way in which money may be found to pay into the Imperial Exchequer the annual charges for loans. At the present moment a sum of £358,000 a-year is paid by the Imperial Exchequer to Local Bodies throughout the country in aid of local rates. This sum will, after the passing of the Bill, have to be paid out of the revenues of the Irish Legislature, for clause 17 repeals the Act of Parliament which made this sum payable out of the Imperial Exchequer. The Irish Government, if hard pressed for money, will not pay these grants in aid at all; the local rates will go up, and every householder in the country will have to put his hand in his pocket in order to meet the necessary increase in taxation.

COURT OF EXCHEQUER.

Exchequer Judges.

Clause 19 of the Bill shows the small amount of confidence which Mr. Gladstone puts in the new Irish Legislature and in the Irish Judges. He proposes to appoint two Judges to form a Court of Exchequer, before whom all "*proceedings instituted by or against the Imperial Treasury, or the Commissioners of Customs, or any of their Officers, or which relate to the election of Members to serve in the Imperial Parliament* (an Election Petition, for instance), *or which touch any matter affected by a law which the Irish Legislature have not power to alter or repeal*," shall be heard and determined if so required by any party to the proceedings. That is to say, the Government of Great Britain will not trust the Judges appointed under the new Irish Legislature to dispense

Their power. justice and to decide according to the law. These Exchequer Judges will be appointed and paid by the Imperial Exchequer, and they are to have power, if their decrees are not duly enforced by the sheriff, to appoint a special officer to carry them out, and such special officer, and all persons employed by him, are to be entitled to all the privileges and powers of the sheriff. The curious state of things which would probably arise under this clause is worth considering. The Court of Exchequer makes a decree, and calls upon the sheriff—of the County of Waterford, for instance—to execute it. The sheriff, who will be in no wise interested in helping the Imperial Government, but rather the reverse, refuses. The Court then appoints a special officer. He calls out the police, but the sheriff forbids them to act. There would then practically be two sheriffs in the county, each with full power, pulling against one another. How would such a deadlock be likely to end? The sheriff of the United Kingdom, if such a dignified title may be given to the officer of the Court of Exchequer, could, of course, call out the military, but probably his legal right to do so would not be one whit greater than that of his antagonist. If men were shot under such circumstances, it is probable that the Exchequer officer would be arrested by the Irish Courts, and put on his trial for murder before a Jury, who would certainly find him guilty. What would the Government of the United Kingdom do in such a condition of things?

Under clause 19, sub-clause 4, any person will have the power to go before the Exchequer Judges to have it declared whether an Act passed by the Irish Legislature, which affects the suitor, comes within its power under the Bill. It is doubtful, however, whether the Legislature, would pay any heed to an adverse decision, and if it did not, the United Kingdom could only enforce the decisions of the Court by employing the army. Probably, rather than get into a deadlock with the Irish Government, the Imperial Government would probably give way, and thus the restrictive clauses would at once become valueless.

Right of private persons to appeal to them.

These Exchequer Judges are really set up for the purpose of safeguarding the interests of the United Kingdom, and yet Ireland has, under the 3rd schedule, to contribute her quota to their salaries. It is unnecessary to dwell on the unfairness of such an arrangement.

THE POST OFFICE.

Post Office.   The 20th clause of the Bill provides that after the "*appointed day the Postal and Telegraph Service in Ireland shall be transferred to the Irish Government, and may be regulated by Irish Act,*" with certain exceptions.

By the Bill of 1886 the Imperial Government proposed to keep the Post Office in its own hands. It was enumerated in clause 3 as one of the subjects with which the Irish Government were not to deal. But in the Bill of 1886 Mr. Gladstone demanded a somewhat larger imperial contribution from Ireland than he asks now in the Bill of 1893. There is, however, an annual loss on the Irish Post Office— a loss amounting to about £50,000 per annum—and in order to recoup himself somewhat for his more moderate demands, the unprofitable Irish Post Office is handed over to the already overburdened Irish Government.

If there is one department of state more than another which should be kept in the hands of the central Government it is the Post Office. Both in the United States, in Germany, in Canada, and in Switzerland the Post Office is an Imperial concern, and the inconvenience which would arise if it were not so, would be enormous. The Irish Legislature will not have the power to change the postal rates for the carriage of letters, or papers, or parcels, or for the transmission of telegrams ; but the Imperial Parliament will be able to reduce the postal rates, and thus cause an additional loss to the Irish Exchequer. Stamps bought in Ireland will no longer be good in England, and stamps bought in England will be worthless in Ireland. Nothing in the whole Bill will give the ordinary man such a sense of the separation of the two countries as this—a separation which, from a national point of view, will be worthless, which will please nobody, because it will injure everybody. The whole tendency of modern international politics is to centralize the Post Office—centralize it even as between otherwise independent states—and this simply because of the great inconvenience caused by having different postal rates and arrangements in small areas. Mr. Gladstone, in this Bill, proposes to take a most retrograde step, which will be injurious alike to Great Britain and Ireland ; and all because he thinks he can saddle the loss of £50,000 *a-year* on the Exchequer of the poorer country, and so allow the Imperial Budget to show an additional profit on the Imperial Post Office. (The profits last year were over £3,000,000, and it might be argued that, as a partner, Ireland is entitled to a share in this sum in proportion to her wealth and population.)

POST OFFICE AND TRUSTEE SAVINGS BANKS.

Clause 21 provides that on *the appointed day* all the Post Office and Trustee Savings Banks in Ireland shall be transferred over to the Irish Government. Every depositor in a Post Office Savings Bank may, if he wishes, before that date, have his deposit repaid to him, or transferred to a Post Office Savings Bank in Great Britain, and all trustees of Trustee Savings Banks may, if they so request, have all sums due to them repaid, and the Banks closed. After that date depositors and trustees will cease to have any claim whatever against the Imperial Government, and the *only security they will have for their money will be the Government of Ireland.* Considering the difficulty which that Government will have in raising sufficient money to carry on its own business, the security can hardly be called a good one.

Post Office
Savings
Banks.
Trustee
Savings
Banks.

IRISH APPEALS.

Clause 22 provides that all appeals from any Court in Ireland to the House of Lords shall cease, and that in future all appeals must be made to the Judicial Committee of the Privy Council. Appeals from all British Colonies or Dependencies are now heard by the Privy Council and not by the House of Lords, and the attempt to put Ireland in the same position as one of the Colonies, while from a practical point it may do her no great harm, is yet one of those subtle provisions which abound throughout the Bill, which must tend in the future towards political and social separation.

Appeals.

THE JUDICIAL COMMITTEE OF THE PRIVY COUNCIL.

Clause 23 will give the Lord Lieutenant or a Secretary of
State power, if he thinks that the Irish Legislature has
exceeded its power, to bring the question before the Judicial
Committee of the English Privy Council for decision. The
Privy Council will thus become a Supreme Court for the inter-
pretation of the Act, and of all constitutional questions
between the two countries. It will take the place of the
Supreme Court in the United States, but with this difference,
that while the Supreme Court in America is in a sense a
part of the Constitution itself, which has grown up and
strengthened with its growth, and which possesses at the
present moment the confidence and respect of every American
citizen, the Privy Council will neither be believed in nor
looked to with confidence by any Irishman. It will be a
body in which there will be but one Irish Judge, sitting in the
capital of a country with which Ireland will be on terms of the
merest toleration, and the natural suspicion of Irishmen will
tend to make them disbelieve in its loyalty to the arrangement entered into, whenever it becomes injurious to the
interests of Great Britain. The decisions of the English
Privy Council will, in all probability, be regarded in Ireland
as so much waste paper, and only armed intervention will be
able to prevent them from being treated as such. In America,
if a State refused to obey the Supreme Court the federal troops
would have to be called in. It may occur sometime or other
on the other side of the Atlantic. It is certain to occur on
this side.

JUDGES AND CIVIL SERVANTS.

Judges.

Clauses 26 to 29 deal with the Judges and the civil servants
generally. The Irish Government will, after the passing of
the Bill, have power to fill up all vacancies which occur in
the Judiciary or in the Civil Services. It will also have power,
after six years, to increase or diminish their salaries at
pleasure, to decrease or increase their number, and, in

fact, to deal with all positions and places under the Crown as it may think fit. The only limit to its power will be the same limit which now exists to the power of the Imperial Parliament, namely, that no Judge shall be dismissed except in pursuance of an address from the two Houses to Her Majesty, and that, whilst they continue in office neither their salaries nor their right to pension shall be diminished without their consent. All existing Judges, save the two Exchequer Judges, who are excepted from the section, and all other officers whose salaries are charged on the Consolidated Fund of the United Kingdom, are to continue as they are at present, and " *to be removable only in the same manner as heretofore,*" and their salaries and pensions are to be paid out of the Irish Consolidated Fund, and, so far as they are not paid out of this Fund, they are to be paid out of the Exchequer of the United Kingdom; and any payment so made shall, on a certificate of the Controller-General of the United Kingdom, countersigned by the Lord Lieutenant, be a charge on the Irish Exchequer. Evidently the framers of the Bill were afraid that some of the Judges would not get their salaries from the Irish Consolidated Fund. They probably knew that some of them were very unpopular with the National Party. Feeling that the honour of Great Britain was at stake in the matter, they guarded the interests of these officers of the United Kingdom by providing, that so far as they were not paid out of the Consolidated Fund of Ireland, they were to be paid by the Exchequer of the United Kingdom. As, however, Great Britain might lose some money if no further arrangements were made, the whole sum so paid is made a first charge on the Irish Exchequer.

Besides the Judges there are very few officers whose salaries are charged on the Consolidated Fund, and who are removable by address. The great mass of the *permanent civil servants of the Crown* hold their offices " at pleasure," that is they are liable at any moment to dismissal. It is beyond doubt that they would be dismissed by the Irish Government in great numbers, without gratuities or pensions of any sort, if the Act did not make some provision for

Permanent Civil Servants.

them. The language held by Nationalists during the last six years has been unmistakable. They intend to fill every office, high and low, with their adherents, and, indeed, no matter what good intentions the leaders may now have, the pressure from behind would, after the passing of the Bill, be too great for them. There are thousands of needy men throughout the country whose one idea is not so much "Home Rule," as "the places which are to be got under Home Rule." In order to meet this wholesale dismissal, which even the framers of the Bill evidently thought would take place, it is provided by clause 28, that for the first three years all the salaries of the permanent civil servants shall be paid out of the Exchequer of the United Kingdom (to be repaid in this case also by the Irish Exchequer, and as a first charge thereon, before any money is paid out for any Irish purposes whatever). It is further provided that after three years any officer may retire from office, *and shall, at any time during those three years, if required by the Irish Government, retire from office*, and that on his doing so the Treasury may award him a gratuity (commutation) or a pension, in accordance with the 5th schedule to the Bill. As this schedule is still blank, it is impossible to know as yet whether the Government intend to deal fairly with the civil servants. As it is pretty certain that a large number of civil servants will resign at the end of three years to avoid being forcibly ejected, it seems probable that the amount of the gratuities and pensions to be paid under the clause will be large, and where the Irish Government (for they will, under sub-clause 5, have to repay the Treasury of the United Kingdom all payments made for gratuities and pensions) will be able to find the money, it is hard, considering their other difficulties, to say.

Gratuities and Pensions.

Existing Pensions.

All existing pensions are to be charged on the Irish Consolidated Fund. If not paid out of that fund they are to be paid by the Exchequer of the United Kingdom, and repaid afterwards in the same way as all other payments by the Irish Exchequer.

Whether all the above payments will be made as directed

is a matter concerning which there is the gravest doubt. If the Irish Government refused to pay them it would be a matter of extreme difficulty to enforce payment. The machinery is lacking, and the army would have to be employed.

THE POLICE.

Clause 30 deals with the Royal Irish Constabulary and the Dublin Metropolitan Police. *Royal Irish Constabulary.*

Dublin Metropolitan Police.

After the passing of the Bill *no officer or man is to be appointed to either force.* For *six years* after the passing of the Bill the Lord Lieutenant is empowered, if he shall consider it expedient, to keep on foot the two forces, but at the end of six years they will, by virtue of the Act, cease to exist. During those six years the Irish Government may establish such local police forces as they think proper, and whenever the Executive Committee of the Irish Privy Council certifies to the Lord Lieutenant that a police force adequate for local purposes has been established in any town or county, then he may, within six months after such certificate, withdraw the Royal Irish Constabulary from such town or county. Similar provisions are made with regard to the Dublin Metropolitan Police. The Lord Lieutenant may further reduce the whole number of the force, proportionately to the number withdrawn from any district.

The powers given into the hands of the Irish Government by this clause are tremendous. It might, if it desired to overawe Ulster, appoint and equip a military police and draft them in large numbers into the north-eastern counties for the purpose of dragooning the malcontents. Further, it might, and the eventuality is by no means impossible, arm every man in the Southern provinces, and pass a law disarming Ulster, or rather the Ulster of the Settlement— Antrim, Down, Armagh, and Derry—and might use the police for the purpose of such disarmament, relying, if necessary, on the Southerns to back them up. It is not suggested that the Irish Government would attempt such a thing as this at once, or would even desire to attempt it; but let blood be roused, let a real pretext be given either by Ulster remaining *Military Police.*

irreconcilable, or by an outburst of Orangeism, and, almost for their own safety, the Home Rule Government would have to take some such strong measures.

Another difficulty might occur. Ireland might be very much disturbed during some part or even during the whole of the first six years. The Lord Lieutenant might not feel himself justified in decreasing the strength of the Constabulary, and in the meantime there would be a second force to be paid. Where is the money to come from ; for the Irish Government assuredly will not have it ?

Expenses.

The dangers which may accrue under this clause by the discharging of the Royal Irish Constabulary, and by giving the police into the hands of the Irish Government, are real and manifold enough to make all Unionists throughout the country tremble at the mere thought of the Bill becoming law.

Pensions.

The schedule to this clause, dealing with the gratuities and pensions to be paid to the police, is still blank ; but whatever they may be finally settled at, Ireland will have to pay two-thirds of the amount. The present cost of the two forces is £1,500,000 per annum. £500,000 of this will, under the 30th clause, be paid by the United Kingdom, and as the police are to be gradually dismissed, this payment will gradually decrease in amount. This is what Mr. Gladstone referred to when he spoke of the £500,000 being a " vanishing amount."

MISCELLANEOUS PROVISIONS.

Clauses 31 to 34 of the Bill are called " Miscellaneous." Why they have been all grouped under such a title it is hard to understand, for two at least of the clauses (namely, 32 and 33) would far more properly come under the headings, " Constitution of the Legislature " (clauses 6 to 8) and " Legislative Authority " (clauses 1 to 4).

Election laws.

Clause 32 provides that *all existing election laws relating to the House of Commons and the Members thereof shall, so far as applicable, extend to each of the two Houses of the Irish Legislature and the Members thereof, but such election laws so far as thereby extended may be altered by Irish Act.* In other words, everything connected with the registration of electors, with the manner of conducting elections and the taking of the poll, the questioning of elections and of corrupt and illegal practices will be handed over to the Irish Legislature. They could, for instance, repeal or radically alter the Ballot Act.

Clause 33 has been already alluded to. It gives the Irish Legislature power to repeal or alter any provision of the Bill which is by the Bill itself made alterable, and also to repeal or alter any enactments in force in Ireland, except such as either relate to matters beyond the powers of the Irish Legislature, *or which, having been enacted by Parliament after the passing of the Bill may be extended to Ireland.* Supremacy of Imperial Parliament.

This is one of the most extraordinary clauses of this extraordinary Bill, and it seems as if it had been shoved in among a number of miscellaneous clauses in order that its true significance might be hidden. It corresponds in part to one of the restrictive sub-clauses of clause 4 of the Bill of 1886 (namely, that one which forbade any alteration in the Bill, save where it was declared alterable), and in part is new. It gives powers of a most enormous kind to the Irish Legislature in one sentence, and makes them all void in the next. To put an extreme case, the Irish Legislature might occupy itself in repealing almost every Act of Parliament dealing with Ireland since Magna Charta down, for the purpose of divesting the law of Ireland of its "foreign garb," but it would be liable to be interrupted in its beneficent labours by an Act of the Imperial Parliament enacting in so many words, "that the Irish Legislative Assembly and Legislative Council be not allowed to sit save during the month of January of every second year." After that the Irish Legislative bodies could not legally sit except during the one month in every two years.

Clause 33, sub-clause 3, will prevent the Irish Legislature from interfering with Bills of Divorce. There is, at the present time, no Law of Divorce in Ireland, and the only way of obtaining a complete separation between husband and wife is by presenting a Bill of Divorce to the House of Lords. This clause forbids the Irish Legislature from taking away Laws relating to Marriage and Divorce.

this right from the Queen's subjects in Ireland, but otherwise it will be able to deal with the marriage laws as it pleases. It might pass a " deceased wife's sister Bill"; might make all mixed marriages illegal or decree that no such marriage should be valid which was not celebrated in the presence of a priest of the Church of Rome, and might make it unnecessary to comply with the present registration laws in the case of a marriage by a Roman Catholic priest.

Under clause 33 great and difficult constitutional questions would be sure to arise which must occupy the time of the Parliament in Westminster.

Clause 31 applies the existing laws relating to the Exchequer in England to the Irish Exchequer, and gives the Lord Lieutenant power to appoint an Irish Comptroller-General. Clause 34 limits the borrowing power of local authorities.

TRANSITORY PROVISIONS.

Clauses 35 to 38 are transitory provisions, that is, they will only be operative for a fixed time.

Irish Land.

Clause 35 provides that for three years from the passing of the Bill into law the Irish Legislature shall not pass an Act respecting the relations of " *landlord and tenant, or the sale, purchase, or letting of land generally.*" This safeguard for the landlords is of the flimsiest and most ridiculous nature. It cannot do them any good, and may do them harm. During those three years it will be in the power of the Irish Government to refuse to enforce the payment of rent, and, if we may judge from the last fourteen years, no rent will, during that time, be paid throughout the country. The landlords will, probably, at the end of that time, be almost all bankrupt, and ready to accept whatever offers may be made to them by the Government. This section is one of the worst and most cruel in a Bill, which, from beginning to end, is ruthless.

Judges to be appointed by Imperial Parliament for six years.

Clause 35, sub-clause 2, provides that for six years the Judges of the Supreme Court in Ireland shall be appointed by Her Majesty as heretofore. If it is safe now to hand over the appointment of the Judges to the Irish Legislature, such a provision as this is merely vexatious; if it is dangerous now, it is hardly likely to become safe within the short period of six years. There is no provision in the Act setting forth by whom or in what manner the Judges are to be appointed, and the Irish Legislature will therefore, after six years, have full power to make the appointment popular— that is, they may decree that the Judges be appointed by a vote of the Legislative Assembly without ratification by the Council, or even by a direct vote of the people themselves. For instance, the County Court Judges might be appointed by the majority of voting ratepayers in a county.

Clause 36 gives to "Her Majesty the Queen in Council" power to make *all* provisional arrangements for the summoning of the Irish Legislative body, and for transferring to the Lord Lieutenant, or to an officer of the Irish Executive Government, rights which now reside in the Queen herself, as head of the Privy Council, for the purpose of adapting them to the new conditions of affairs.

Clause 37 provides that, save where otherwise provided, all existing laws, institutions, authorities and officers in Ireland, and all existing taxes shall continue as if the Act had not passed. The section is, of course, subject to the powers given to the new Legislature of making any changes they may think proper.

Clause 38 says that the "*appointed day*" on which the new arrangements are to commence shall be the day of the first meeting of the Irish Legislature, or such other day not more than *seven months* earlier or later, as may be fixed upon by Her Majesty in Council, and that different days may be appointed for different purposes and different provisions of the Bill.

Appointed day.

Clause 39 defines a number of words and expressions used in the Bill, and clause 40 says that the Bill may be cited as the "Irish Government Act, 1893."

In considering the Bill, as a whole, three things stand out with special prominence :—Firstly, its complexity; secondly, its want of any definite principle; thirdly, its want of finality. With regard to the first—its complexity—that has been sufficiently demonstrated by the foregoing remarks. As to its want of principle, that is shown by the way in which powers are given by one section in order to please one set of people, and then withdrawn in order to meet the views of another set; and by the way in which restrictions are introduced to meet the views of the Loyalists, and then made illusory in order to prevent the Nationalists complaining. The Bill is uncandid and cowardly. It trusts no one, shows confidence in no one. It was meant to catch the unthinking of every party, and will eventually please none. It is not in the nature of a compromise, for there is no "give and take" about it. For the purpose of avoiding objections, and passing it easily through Parliament, it has purposely been left vague in its language, and the consequence will be, if it ever becomes law, that constitutional disputes of immense magnitude and extremely difficult to solve, will arise under almost every section.

Lastly, as to its "want of finality," the Bill cannot satisfy the Nationalist sentiment which it purports to recognize, for, under it, Ireland will be, not a nation, but a subordinate province. It will not satisfy those who hope, by means of a National Legislature, to make the country prosperous, for it will create a Government without means and without credit. Finally, it cannot satisfy Great Britain, for instead of freeing the Imperial Parliament from the pressure of the Irish difficulty, it must create in Westminster a new and more intense Irish question than that which it professes to settle.

APPENDIX.

GOVERNMENT OF IRELAND BILL,
1893.

ARRANGEMENT OF CLAUSES.

PART I.

A BILL

TO AMEND

A D. 1893. *The provision for the Government of Ireland,* 1893.

[56 VICT.]

WHEREAS it is expedient that without impairing or restricting the supreme authority of Parliament, an Irish
Legislature should be created for such purposes in Ireland as in
this Act mentioned :

Be it therefore enacted by the Queen's most Excellent
Majesty, by and with the advice and consent of the Lords
Spiritual and Temporal, and Commons, in this present Parlia-
ment assembled, and by the authority of the same, as follows :

PART I.

Legislative Authority.

Establish-
ment of
Irish Legis-
lature.

1. *On and after the appointed day* there shall be in Ireland a
Legislature consisting of Her Majesty the Queen and of two
Houses, the Legislative Council and the Legislative Assembly.

Powers of
Irish Legis-
lature.

2. With the exceptions and subject to the restrictions in this
Act mentioned, there shall be granted to the Irish Legislature
power to make laws for the peace, order, and good government
of Ireland in respect of matters exclusively relating to Ireland
or some part thereof.

Exceptions
from powers
of Irish
Legislature.

3. The Irish Legislature shall not have power to make laws
in respect of the following matters or any of them :—

    (1.) The Crown, or the succession to the Crown, or a Regency ;
        or the Lord Lieutenant as representative of the Crown ;
        or

    (2.) The making of peace or war or matters arising from a
        state of war ; or

    (3.) Naval or military forces, or the defence of the realm ; or

    (4.) Treaties and other relations with foreign States or the
        relations between different parts of Her Majesty's
        dominions or offences connected with such treaties or
        relations ; or

A.D. 1893.

(5.) Dignities or titles of honour ; or

(6.) Treason, treason-felony, alienage, or naturalization ; or

(7.) Trade with any place out of Ireland ; or quarantine, or navigation (except as respects inland waters and local health or harbour regulations) ; or

(8.) Beacons, lighthouses, or sea marks (except so far as they can consistently with any general Act of Parliament be constructed or maintained by a local harbour authority) ; or

(9.) Coinage ; legal tender ; or the standard of weights and measures ; or

(10.) Trade marks, merchandise marks, copyright, or patent rights.

Any law made in contravention of this section shall be void.

4. The powers of the Irish Legislature shall not extend to the making of any law—

Restrictions on powers of Irish Legislature.

(1.) Respecting the establishment or endowment of religion, or prohibiting the free exercise thereof ; or

(2.) Imposing any disability, or conferring any privilege, on account of religious belief ; or

(3.) Abrogating or prejudicially affecting the right to establish or maintain any place of denominational education or any denominational institution or charity ; or

(4.) Prejudicially affecting the right of any child to attend a school receiving public money, without attending the religious instruction at that school ; or

(5.) Whereby any person may be deprived of life, liberty, or property without due process of law, or may be denied the equal protection of the laws, or whereby private property may be taken without just compensation ; or

(6.) Whereby any existing corporation incorporated by Royal Charter or by any local or general Act of Parliament (not being a corporation raising for public purposes taxes, rates, cess, dues, or tolls, or administering funds so raised) may, unless it consents, or the leave of Her Majesty is first obtained on address from the two Houses of the Irish Legislature, be deprived of its rights, privileges, or property without due process of law ; or

(7.) Whereby any inhabitant of the United Kingdom may be deprived of equal rights as respects public sea fisheries.

Any law made in contravention of this section shall be void.

A.D. 1893.

——

Executive Authority.

Executive
power in
Ireland.

5.—(1.) The executive power in Ireland shall continue vested in Her Majesty the Queen, and the Lord Lieutenant, on behalf of Her Majesty, shall exercise any prerogatives or other executive power of the Queen the exercise of which may be delegated to him by Her Majesty, and shall, in Her Majesty's name, summon, prorogue, and dissolve the Irish Legislature.

(2.) There shall be an Executive Committee of the Privy Council of Ireland to aid and advise in the government of Ireland, being of such numbers, and comprising persons holding such offices, as Her Majesty may think fit, or as may be directed by Irish Act.

(3.) The Lord Lieutenant shall, on the advice of the said Executive Committee, give or withhold the assent of Her Majesty to Bills passed by the two Houses of the Irish Legislature, subject nevertheless to any instructions given by Her Majesty in respect of any such Bill.

Constitution of Legislature.

Composition
of Irish
Legislative
Council.

6.—(1.) The Irish Legislative Council shall consist of *forty-eight* councillors.

(2.) Each of the constituencies mentioned in the First Schedule to this Act shall return the number of councillors named opposite thereto in that schedule.

(3.) Every man shall be entitled to be registered as an elector, and when registered to vote at an election, of a councillor for a constituency, who owns or occupies any land or tenement in the constituency of a rateable value of more than *twenty* pounds, subject to the like conditions as a man is entitled at the passing of this Act to be registered and vote as a parliamentary elector in respect of an ownership qualification or of the qualification

48 & 49 Vict.
c. 3.

specified in section five of the Representation of the People Act, 1884, as the case may be: Provided that a man shall not be entitled to be registered, nor if registered to vote, at an election of a councillor in more than one constituency in the same year.

(4.) The term of office of every councillor shall be *eight* years, and shall not be affected by a dissolution; and one *half* of the councillors shall retire in every *fourth* year, and their seats shall be filled by a new election.

Composition
of Irish
Legislative
Assembly.

7.—(1.) The Irish Legislative Assembly shall consist of *one hundred and three* members, returned by the existing parliamentary constituencies in Ireland, or the existing divisions thereof, and elected by the parliamentary electors for the time being in those constituencies or divisions.

(2.) The Irish Legislative Assembly when summoned may, unless sooner dissolved, have continuance for *five* years from the day on which the summons directs it to meet and no longer.

(3.) After *six* years from the passing of this Act, the Irish Legislature may alter the qualification of the electors, and the constituencies, and the distribution of the members among the constituencies, provided that in such distribution due regard is had to the population of the constituencies.

8. If a Bill or any provision of a Bill adopted by the Legislative Assembly is lost by the disagreement of the Legislative Council, and after a dissolution, or the period of *two years* from such disagreement, such Bill, or a Bill for enacting the said provision, is again adopted by the Legislative Assembly and fails within three months afterwards to be adopted by the Legislative Council, the same shall forthwith be submitted to the members of the two Houses deliberating and voting together thereon, and shall be adopted or rejected according to the decision of the majority of those members present and voting on the question.

Irish Representation in House of Commons.

9. Unless and until Parliament otherwise determines, the following provisions shall have effect—

(1.) After *the appointed day* each of the constituencies named in the Second Schedule to this Act shall return to serve in Parliament the number of members named opposite thereto in that schedule, and no more, and Dublin University shall cease to return any member.

(2.) The existing divisions of the constituencies shall, save as provided in that schedule, be abolished.

(3.) An Irish representative peer in the House of Lords and a member of the House of Commons for an Irish constituency shall not be entitled to deliberate or vote on—

(a) any Bill or motion in relation thereto, the operation of which Bill or motion is confined to Great Britain or some part thereof ; or

(b) any motion or resolution relating solely to some tax not raised or to be raised in Ireland ; or

(c) any vote or appropriation of money made exclusively for some service not mentioned in the Third Schedule to this Act ; or

(d) any motion or resolution exclusively affecting Great Britain or some part thereof or some local authority or some person or thing therein ; or

(*e*) any motion or resolution, incidental to any such
motion or resolution as either is last mentioned,
or relates solely to some tax not raised or be raised
in Ireland, or incidental to any such vote or appropriation of money as aforesaid.

(4.) Compliance with the provisions of this section shall not
be questioned otherwise than in each House in manner
provided by the House.

(5.) The election laws and the laws relating to the qualification of parliamentary electors shall not, so far as they
relate to parliamentary elections, be altered by the
Irish Legislature, but this enactment shall not prevent
the Irish Legislature from dealing with any officers
concerned with the issue of writs of election, and if
any officers are so dealt with, it shall be lawful for
Her Majesty by Order in Council to arrange for the
issue of such writs, and the writs issued in pursuance
of such Order shall be of the same effect as if issued
in manner heretofore accustomed.

Finance.

As to
separate
Consoli-
dated Fund
and taxes.

10.—(1.) *On and after the appointed day* there shall be an
Irish Exchequer and Consolidated Fund separate from those of
the United Kingdom.

(2.) The duties of customs and excise and the duties on
postage shall be imposed by Act of Parliament, but subject to
the provisions of this Act the Irish Legislature may, in order
to provide for the public service of Ireland, impose any other
taxes.

(3.) Save as in this Act mentioned, all matters relating to
the taxes in Ireland and the collection and management thereof
shall be regulated by Irish Act, and the same shall be collected
and managed by the Irish Government and form part of the
public revenues of Ireland : Provided that—

(*a*) the duties of customs shall be regulated, collected, managed,
and paid into the Exchequer of the United Kingdom
as heretofore ; and

(*b*) all prohibitions in connexion with the duties of excise,
and so far as regards articles sent out of Ireland, all
matters relating to those duties, shall be regulated by
Act of Parliament ; and

(*c*) the excise duties on articles consumed in Great Britain
shall be paid in Great Britain or to an officer of the
Government of the United Kingdom.

(4.) Save as in this Act mentioned, all the public revenues

of Ireland shall be paid into the Irish Exchequer and form a
Consolidated Fund, and be appropriated to the public service of
Ireland by Irish Act.

(5.) If the duties of excise are increased above the rates in
force on *the first day of March one thousand eight hundred and
ninety-three,* the net proceeds in Ireland of the duties in excess
of the said rates, shall be paid from the Irish Exchequer to the
Exchequer of the United Kingdom.

(6.) *If the duties of excise are reduced below the rates in force
on the said day, and the net proceeds of such duties in Ireland are
in consequence less than the net proceeds of the duties before the
reduction, a sum equal to the deficiency shall, unless it is otherwise agreed between the Treasury and the Irish Government, be
paid from the Exchequer of the United Kingdom to the Irish
Exchequer.*

11.—(1.) The hereditary revenues of the Crown in Ireland
which are managed by the Commissioners of Woods shall continue during the life of Her present Majesty to be managed
and collected by those Commissioners, and the net amount payable by them to the Exchequer on account of those revenues,
after deducting all expenses (but including an allowance for
interest on such proceeds of the sale of those revenues as have
not been re-invested in Ireland), shall be paid into the Treasury
Account (Ireland) herein-after mentioned, for the benefit of the
Irish Exchequer.

Hereditary revenues and income tax.

(2.) A person shall not be required to pay income tax in
Great Britain in respect of property situate or business carried
on in Ireland, and a person shall not be required to pay income
tax in Ireland in respect of property situate or business carried
on in Great Britain.

(3.) *For the purpose of giving to Ireland the benefit of the difference between the income tax collected in Great Britain from
British, Colonial, and foreign securities held by residents in Ireland, and the income tax collected in Ireland from Irish securities
held by residents in Great Britain, there shall be made to Ireland
out of the income tax collected in Great Britain, an allowance of
such amount as may be from time to time determined by the Treasury, in accordance with a minute of the Treasury laid before
Parliament before the appointed day, and such allowance shall be
paid into the Treasury Account (Ireland) for the benefit of the
Irish Exchequer.*

(4.) Provided that the provisions of this section with respect
to income tax shall not apply to any excess of the rate of income
tax in Great Britain above the rate in Ireland or of the rate of
income tax in Ireland above the rate in Great Britain.

A.D. 1893.

Financial
arrange-
ments as
between
United
Kingdom
and Ireland.

12.—(1.) The duties of customs contributed by Ireland and, save as provided by this Act, that portion of any public revenue of the United Kingdom to which Ireland may claim to be entitled, whether specified in the Third Schedule to this Act or not, shall be carried to the Consolidated Fund of the United Kingdom, as the contribution of Ireland to Imperial liabilities and expenditure as defined in that Schedule.

(2.) The civil charges of the Government in Ireland shall, subject as in this Act mentioned, be borne after the appointed day by Ireland.

(3.) After *fifteen* years from the passing of this Act the arrangements made by this Act for the contribution of Ireland to Imperial liabilities and expenditure, and otherwise for the financial relations between the United Kingdom and Ireland, may be revised in pursuance of an address to Her Majesty from the House of Commons, or from the Irish Legislative Assembly.

13.—(1.) There shall be established under the direction of the Treasury an account (in this Act referred to as the Treasury Account (Ireland).

(2.) There shall be paid into such account all sums payable from the Irish Exchequer to the Exchequer of the United Kingdom, or from the latter to the former Exchequer, and all sums directed to be paid into the account for the benefit of either of the said Exchequers.

(3.) All sums, which are payable from either of the said Exchequers to the other of them, or being payable out of one of the said Exchequers are repayable by the other Exchequer, shal in the first instance be payable out of the said account so far as the money standing on the account is sufficient ; and for the purpose of meeting such sums, the Treasury out of the customs revenue collected in Ireland, and the Irish Government out of any of the public revenues in Ireland, may direct money to be paid to the Treasury Account (Ireland) instead of into the Exchequer.

(4.) Any surplus standing on the account to the credit of either Exchequer, and not required for meeting payments, shall at convenient times be paid into that Exchequer, and where any sum so payable into the Exchequer of the United Kingdom is required by law to be forthwith paid to the National Debt Commissioners, that sum may be paid to those Commissioners without being paid into the Exchequer.

(5.) All sums payable by virtue of this Act out of the Consolidated Fund of the United Kingdom or of Ireland shall be payable from the Exchequer of the United Kingdom or Ireland, as the case may be, within the meaning of this Act, and all sums by this Act made payable from the Exchequer of the

United Kingdom shall, if not otherwise paid, be charged on and
paid out of the Consolidated Fund of the United Kingdom.

14.—(1.) There shall be charged on the Irish Consolidated Charges on
Fund in favour of the Exchequer of the United Kingdom as a solidated
first charge on that fund all sums which— Fund.

(*a*) are payable to that Exchequer from the Irish Exchequer ;
or

(*b*) are required to repay to the Exchequer of the United
Kingdom sums issued to meet the dividends or sinking
fund on guaranteed land stock under the Purchase of 54 & 55 Vict.
Land (Ireland) Act, 1891, or c. 48.

(*c*) otherwise have been or are required to be paid out of the
Exchequer of the United Kingdom in consequence of
the non-payment thereof out of the Exchequer of
Ireland or otherwise by the Irish Government.

(2.) If at any time the Controller and Auditor General of the
United Kingdom is satisfied that any such charge is due, he
shall certify the amount of it, and the Treasury shall send such
certificate to the Lord Lieutenant, who shall thereupon by order
without any counter-signature, direct the payment of the
amount from the Irish Exchequer to the Exchequer of the
United Kingdom, and such order shall be duly obeyed by all
persons, and until the amount is wholly paid no other payment
shall be made out of the Irish Exchequer for any purpose whatever.

(3.) There shall be charged on the Irish Consolidated Fund
next after the foregoing charge ;

(*a*) all sums, for dividends or sinking fund on guaranteed
land stock under the Purchase of Land (Ireland) Act, 54 & 55 Vict.
1891, which the Land Purchase Account and the c. 48.
Guarantee Fund under that Act are insufficient to pay ;

(*b*) all sums due in respect of any debt incurred by the
Government of Ireland, whether for interest, management, or sinking fund ;

(*c*) an annual sum of *five thousand* pounds for the expenses of
the household and establishment of the Lord Lieutenant ;

(*d*) all existing charges on the Consolidated Fund of the
United Kingdom in respect of Irish services other
than the salary of the Lord Lieutenant ; and

(*e*) the salaries and pensions of all judges of the Supreme
Court or other superior court in Ireland or of any
county or other like court, who are appointed after
the passing of this Act, and are not the Exchequer
judges hereafter mentioned.

48   *The Government of Ireland Bill, 1893.*

A.D. 1893.

(4.) Until all charges created by this Act upon the Irish Consolidated Fund and for the time being due are paid, no money shall be issued from the Irish Exchequer for any other purpose whatever.

Irish Church Fund.
32 & 33 Vict. c. 42.
44 & 45 Vict. c. 71.

15.—(1.) All existing charges on the Church property in Ireland,—that is to say, all property accruing under the Irish Church Act, 1869, and transferred to the Irish Land Commission by the Irish Church Amendment Act, 1881—shall so far as not paid out of the said property be charged on the Irish Consolidated Fund, and any of those charges guaranteed by the Treasury, if and so far as not paid, shall be paid out of the Exchequer of the United Kingdom.

(2.) Subject to the existing charges thereon, the said Church property shall belong to the Irish Government, and be managed, administered, and disposed of as directed by Irish Act.

Local loans.

16.—(1.) All sums paid or applicable in or towards the discharge of the interest or principal of any local loan advanced before the appointed day on security in Ireland, or otherwise in respect of such loan, which but for this Act would be paid to the National Debt Commissioners, and carried to the Local Loans Fund shall, after the appointed day, be paid, until otherwise provided by Irish Act, to the Irish Exchequer.

(2.) For the payment to the Local Loans Fund of the principal and interest of such loans, the Irish Government shall after the appointed day pay by half yearly payments an annuity for *forty-nine* years, at the rate of *four* per cent on the principal of the said loans, exclusive of any sums written off before the appointed day from the account of assets of the Local Loans Fund, and such annuity shall be paid from the Irish Exchequer to the Exchequer of the United Kingdom, and when so paid shall be forthwith paid to the National Debt Commissioners for the credit of the Local Loans Fund.

(3.) After the appointed day, money for loans in Ireland shall cease to be advanced either by the Public Works Loan Commissioners or out of the Local Loans Fund.

Adaptation of Acts as to Local Taxation Accounts and probate, &c. duties.
See 50 & 51 Vict. c. 41.
54 & 55 Vict. c. 48.

17.—(1.) So much of any Act as directs payment to the Local Taxation (Ireland) Account of any share of probate excise or customs duties payable to the Exchequer of the United Kingdom shall, together with any enactment amending the same, be repealed as from the appointed day without prejudice to the adjustment of balances after that day; but the like amounts shall continue to be paid to the Local Taxation Accounts in England and Scotland as would have been paid if this Act had not passed, and any residue of the said share shall be paid into the Exchequer of the United Kingdom.

(2.) The stamp duty chargeable in respect of the personalty

of a deceased person, shall not in the case of administration A.D. 1893.
granted in Great Britain be chargeable in respect of any
personalty situate in Ireland, nor in the case of administration
granted in Ireland be chargeable in respect of any personalty
situate in Great Britain ; and any administration granted in
Great Britain shall not, if re-sealed in Ireland, be exempt from
stamp duty on administration granted in Ireland, and any
administration granted in Ireland shall not, when re-sealed in
Great Britain, be exempt from stamp duty on administration
granted in Great Britain.

See 21 & 22 Vict. c. 86. ss. 12-18. 21 & 22 Vict. c. 95. s. 29. 22 & 23 Vict. c. 31. s. 25. 39 & 40 Vict. c.70.ss.41-4.

(3.) In this section the expression "administration" means
probate or letters of administration, and as respects Scotland,
confirmation inclusive of the inventory required under the Acts
relating to the said stamp duty, and the expression "personalty"
means personal or moveable estate and effects.

18.—(1.) Bills for appropriating any part of the public
revenue or for imposing any tax shall originate in the Legislative Assembly.

Money bills and votes.

(2.) It shall not be lawful for the Legislative Assembly to
adopt or pass any vote, resolution, address, or Bill for the
appropriation for any purpose of any part of the public revenue
of Ireland, or of any tax, except in pursuance of a recommendation from the Lord Lieutenant in the session in which such
vote, resolution, address, or Bill is proposed.

19.—(1.) Two of the judges of the Supreme Court in Ireland shall be Exchequer judges, and shall be appointed under
the great seal of the United Kingdom ; and their salaries and
pensions shall be charged on and paid out of the Consolidated
Fund of the United Kingdom.

Exchequer judges for revenue actions, election petitions, &c.

(2.) The Exchequer judges shall be removeable only by Her
Majesty on address from the two Houses of Parliament, and
each such judge shall, save as otherwise provided by Parliament, receive the same salary and be entitled to the same
pension as is at the time of his appointment fixed for the puisne
judges of the Supreme Court, and during his continuance in
office his salary shall not be diminished, nor his right to pension
altered, without his consent.

(3.) An alteration of any rules relating to such legal proceedings as are mentioned in this section shall not be made
except with the approval of Her Majesty the Queen in Council ;
and the sittings of the Exchequer judges shall be regulated with
the like approval.

(4.) All legal proceedings in Ireland, which are instituted at
the instance of or against the Treasury or Commissioners of
customs, or any of their officers, or relate to the election of
members to serve in Parliament, or touch any matter not within

A.D. 1893.
———

the powers of the Irish Legislature, or touch any matter affected by a law which the Irish Legislature have not power to repeal or alter, shall, if so required by any party to such proceedings, be heard and determined before the Exchequer judges or (except where the case requires to be determined by two judges) before one of them, and in any such legal proceeding an appeal shall, if any party so requires, lie from any court of first instance in Ireland to the Exchequer judges, and the decision of the Exchequer judges shall be subject to appeal to Her Majesty the Queen in Council and not to any other tribunal.

(5.) If it is made to appear to an Exchequer judge that any decree or judgment in any such proceeding as aforesaid has not been duly enforced by the sheriff or other officer whose duty it is to enforce the same, such judge shall appoint some officer whose duty it shall be to enforce that judgment or decree ; and for that purpose such officer and all persons employed by him shall be entitled to the same privileges, immunities, and powers as are by law conferred on a sheriff and his officers.

(6.) The Exchequer judges, when not engaged in hearing and determining such legal proceedings as above in this section mentioned, shall perform such of the duties ordinarily performed by other judges of the Supreme Court in Ireland as may be assigned by Her Majesty the Queen in Council.

(7.) All sums recovered by the Treasury or the Commissioners of customs or any of their officers, or recovered under any Act relating to duties of customs, shall, notwithstanding anything in any other Act, be paid to such public account as the Treasury or the Commissioners direct.

Post Office Postal Telegraphs and Savings Banks.

Transfer of post office and postal telegraphs.

20.—(1.) As from *the appointed day* the postal and telegraph service in Ireland shall be transferred to the Irish Government, and may be regulated by Irish Act, except as in this Act mentioned and except as regards matters relating—

(*a*) to such conditions of the transmission or delivery of postal packets and telegrams as are incidental to the duties on postage ; or

(*b*) to foreign mails or submarine telegraphs or through lines in connection therewith ; or

(*c*) to any other postal or telegraphic business in connection with places out of the United Kingdom.

(2.) The administration of or incidental to the said excepted matters shall, save as may be otherwise arranged with the Irish Post Office remain with the Postmaster-General.

(3.) As regards the revenue and expenses of the postal and

telegraph service, the Postmaster-General shall retain the A.D. 1893. revenue collected and defray the expenses incurred in Great Britain, and the Irish Post Office shall retain the revenue collected and defray the expenses incurred in Ireland, subject to the provisions of the Fourth Schedule to this Act; which schedule shall have full effect, but may be varied or added to by agreement between the Postmaster-General and the Irish Post Office.

(4) *The sums payable by the Postmaster-General or Irish Post Office to the other of them in pursuance of this Act shall, if not paid out of Post Office moneys, be paid from the Exchequer of the United Kingdom or of Ireland, as the case requires, to the other Exchequer.*

(5.) Sections forty-eight to fifty-two of the Telegraph Act, 26 & 27 Vict c. 112. 1863, and any enactment amending the same, shall apply to all telegraphic lines of the Irish Government in like manner as to the telegraphs of a company within the meaning of that Act.

21.—(1.) As from *the appointed day* there shall be transferred Transfer of savings banks. to the Irish Government the post office savings banks in Ireland and all such powers and duties of any department or officer in Great Britain as are connected with post office savings banks, trustee savings banks or friendly societies in Ireland, and the same may be regulated by Irish Act.

(2.) The Treasury shall publish not less than six months previous notice of the transfer of Savings Banks.

(3.) If before the date of the transfer any depositor in a Post Office Savings Bank so requests, his deposit shall, according to his request either be paid to him or transferred to a Post Office Savings Bank in Great Britain, and after the said date the depositors in a Post Office Savings Bank in Ireland shall cease to have any claim against the Postmaster-General or the Consolidated Fund of the United Kingdom, but shall have the like claim against the Government and Consolidated Fund of Ireland;

(4.) If before the date of the transfer the trustees of any trustee savings bank so request, then, according to the request, either all sums due to them shall be repaid and the savings bank closed, or those sums shall be paid to the Irish Government, and after the said date the trustees shall cease to have any claim against the National Debt Commissioners or the Consolidated Fund of the United Kingdom, but shall have the like claim against the Government and Consolidated Fund of Ireland.

(5.) Notwithstanding the foregoing provisions of this section, if a sum due on account of any annuity or policy of insurance which has before the above-mentioned notice been granted through a Post Office or Trustee Savings Bank, is not paid by the Irish Government, that sum shall be paid out of the Exchequer of the United Kingdom.

Irish Appeals and Decision of Constitutional Questions.

22.—(1.) The appeal from courts in Ireland to the House of Lords shall cease; and where any person would, but for this Act, have a right to appeal from any court in Ireland to the House of Lords, such person shall have the like right to appeal to Her Majesty the Queen in Council; and the right so to appeal shall not be affected by any Irish Act; and all enactments relating to appeals to Her Majesty the Queen in Council, and to the Judicial Committee of the Privy Council, shall apply accordingly.

(2.) When the Judicial Committee sit for hearing appeals from a court in Ireland, there shall be present not less than four Lords of Appeal, within the meaning of the Appellate Jurisdiction Act, 1876, and at least one member who is or has been a judge of the Supreme Court in Ireland.

(3.) A rota of privy councillors to sit for hearing appeals from courts in Ireland shall be made annually by Her Majesty in Council, and the privy councillors, or some of them, on that rota shall sit to hear the said appeals. A casual vacancy in such rota during the year may be filled by Order in Council.

(3.) Nothing in this Act shall affect the jurisdiction of the House of Lords to determine the claims to Irish peerages.

Special
provision for
decision of
constitu-
tional
questions.

23.—(1.) If it appears to the Lord Lieutenant or a Secretary of State expedient in the public interest that steps shall be taken for the speedy determination of the question whether any Irish Act or any provision thereof is beyond the powers of the Irish Legislature, he may represent the same to Her Majesty in Council, and thereupon the said question shall be forthwith referred to and heard and determined by the Judicial Committee of the Privy Council, constituted as if hearing an appeal from a court in Ireland.

(2.) Upon the hearing of the question such persons as seem to the Judicial Committee to be interested may be allowed to appear and be heard as parties to the case, and the decision of the Judicial Committee shall be given in like manner as if it were the decision of an appeal, the nature of the report or recommendation to Her Majesty being stated in open court.

(3.) Nothing in this Act shall prejudice any other power of Her Majesty in Council to refer any question to the Judicial Committee or the right of any person to petition Her Majesty for such reference.

A.D. 1893.

Lord Lieutenant and Crown lands.

24.—(1.) Notwithstanding anything to the contrary in any Act, every subject of the Queen shall be qualified to hold the office of Lord Lieutenant of Ireland, without reference to his religious belief.

(2.) The term of office of the Lord Lieutenant shall be *six years*, without prejudice to the power of Her Majesty the Queen at any time to revoke the appointment.

Office of Lord Lieutenant.

25. Her Majesty the Queen in Council may place under the control of the Irish Government, for the purposes of that Government, such of the lands and buildings in Ireland vested in or held in trust for Her Majesty, and subject to such conditions or restrictions (if any), as may seem expedient.

Use of Crown lands by Irish Government.

Judges and Civil Servants.

26. A judge of the Supreme Court or other superior court in Ireland, or of any county court or other court with a like jurisdiction in Ireland, appointed after the passing of this Act, shall not be removed from his office except in pursuance of an address from the two Houses of the Legislature of Ireland, nor during his continuance in office shall his salary be diminished or right to pension altered without his consent.

Tenure of future judges.

27.—(1.) All existing judges of the Supreme Court, county court judges, and Land Commissioners in Ireland and all existing officers serving in Ireland in the permanent civil service of the Crown and receiving salaries charged on the Consolidated Fund of the United Kingdom, shall, if they are removeable at present on address from both Houses of Parliament, continue to be removeable only upon such address, and if removeable in any other manner shall continue to be removeable only in the same manner as heretofore ; and shall continue to receive the same salaries, gratuities, and pensions, and to be liable to perform the same duties as heretofore, or such duties as Her Majesty may declare to be analogous, and their salaries and pensions, if and so far as not paid out of the Irish Consolidated Fund, shall be paid out of the Exchequer of the United Kingdom : Provided that this section shall be subject to the provisions of this Act with respect to the Exchequer judges.

As to existing judges and other persons having salaries charged on the Consolidated Fund.

(2.) *If any of the said judges, commissioners, or officers retires from office with the Queen's approbation before completion of the period of service entitling him to a pension, Her Majesty may, if she thinks fit, grant to him such pension, not exceeding the pension to which he would on that completion have been entitled, as to Her Majesty seems meet.*

E

A.D. 1893.

As to persons holding civil service appointments.

28.—(1.) All existing officers in the permanent civil service of the Crown, who are not above provided for, and are at the appointed day serving in Ireland, shall after that day continue to hold their offices by the same tenure and to receive the same salaries, gratuities, and pensions, and to be liable to perform the same duties as heretofore or such duties as the Treasury may declare to be analogous; *and the said gratuities and pensions, and until three years after the passing of this Act, the salaries due to any of the said officers if remaining in his existing office, shall be paid to the payees by the Treasury out of the Exchequer of the United Kingdom.*

(2.) Any such officer may after *three years* from the passing of this Act retire from office, and shall, at any time during those three years, if required by the Irish Government, retire from office, and on any such retirement may be awarded by the Treasury a gratuity or pension in accordance with the Fifth Schedule to this Act; Provided that—

(*a*) six months written notice shall, unless it is otherwise agreed, be given either by the said officer or by the Irish Government as the case requires ; and

(*b*) such number of officers only shall retire at one time and at such intervals of time as the Treasury, in communication with the Irish Government, sanction.

(3.) If any such officer does not so retire, the Treasury may award him after the said three years a pension in accordance with the Fifth Schedule to this Act which shall become payable to him on his ultimate retirement from the service of the Crown.

(4.) *The gratuities and pensions awarded in accordance with the Fifth Schedule to this Act shall be paid by the Treasury to the payees out of the Exchequer of the United Kingdom.*

(5.) All sums paid out of the Exchequer of the United Kingdom in pursuance of this section shall be repaid to that Exchequer from the Irish Exchequer.

(6.) This section shall not apply to officers retained in the service of the Government of the United Kingdom.

As to existing pensions and superannuation allowances.

29. Any existing pension granted on account of service in Ireland as a judge of the Supreme Court or of any court consolidated into that court, or as a county court judge, or in any other judicial position, or as an officer in the permanent civil service of the Crown other than in an office the holder of which is after the appointed day retained in the service of the Government of

the United Kingdom, shall be charged on the Irish Consolidated A.D. 1893.
Fund, and if and so far as not paid out of that fund, shall be paid —
out of the Exchequer of the United Kingdom.

Police.

30.—(1.) The forces of the Royal Irish Constabulary and As to
Dublin Metropolitan Police shall, when and as local police forces Police.
are from time to time established in Ireland in accordance with
the Sixth Schedule to this Act, be gradually reduced and ulti-
mately cease to exist as mentioned in that Schedule ; and after
the passing of this Act, no officer or man shall be appointed to
either of those forces ;

Provided that until the expiration of *six* years from the
appointed day, nothing in this Act shall require the Lord Lieutenant to cause either of the said forces to cease to exist, if as
representing Her Majesty the Queen he considers it inexpedient.

(2.) The said two forces shall, while they continue, be subject
to the control of the Lord Lieutenant as representing Her Majesty, and the members thereof shall continue to receive the
same salaries, gratuities, and pensions, and hold their appointments on the same tenure as heretofore, *and those salaries
gratuities, and pensions, and all the expenditure incidental to
either force, shall be paid out of the Exchequer of the United
Kingdom.*

(3.) When any existing member of either force retires under
the provisions of the Sixth Schedule to this Act, the Treasury
may award to him a gratuity or pension in accordance with
that Schedule.

(4.) *Those gratuities and pensions and all existing pensions
payable in respect of service in either force, shall be paid by the
Treasury to the payees out of the Exchequer of the United Kingdom.*

(5.) *Two-thirds of the net amount payable in pursuance of this
section out of the Exchequer of the United Kingdom shall be repaid
to that Exchequer from the Irish Exchequer.*

Miscellaneous.

31. Save as may be otherwise provided by Irish Act,—

(*a*) The existing law relating to the Exchequer and Consoli- Irish
dated Fund of the United Kingdom shall apply with Exchequer
the necessary modifications to the Exchequer and Con- Consoli-
solidated Fund of Ireland, and an officer shall be and Audit.
appointed by the Lord Lieutenant to be the Irish
Comptroller and Auditor General; and

(*b*) The Accounts of the Irish Consolidated Fund shall be
audited as appropriation accounts in manner provided
by the Exchequer and Audit Departments Act, 1866, 29 & 30 Vict.
by or under the direction of such officer. c. 39.

E 2

Law appli-
cable to both
Houses of
Irish Legis-
lature.

32.—(1.) Subject as in this Act mentioned and particularly to the Seventh Schedule to this Act (which Schedule shall have full effect) all existing election laws relating to the House of Commons and the members thereof shall, so far as applicable, extend to each of the two Houses of the Irish Legislature and the members thereof, but such election laws so far as hereby extended may be altered by Irish Act.

(2.) The privileges, rights, and immunities to be held and enjoyed by each House and the members thereof shall be such as may be defined by Irish Act, but so that the same shall never exceed those for the time being held and enjoyed by the House of Commons, and the members thereof.

Supple-
mental
provisions
as to powers
of Irish
Legislature.

33.—(1.) The Irish Legislature may repeal or alter any provision of this Act which is by this Act expressly made alterable by that Legislature, and also any enactments in force in Ireland, except such as either relate to matters beyond the powers of the Irish Legislature, or being enacted by Parliament after the passing of this Act may be expressly extended to Ireland. An Irish Act, notwithstanding it is in any respect repugnant to any enactment excepted as aforesaid, shall, though read subject to that enactment, be, except to the extent of that repugnancy, valid.

(2.) An order, rule, or regulation, made in pursuance of, or having the force of, an Act of Parliament, shall be deemed to be an enactment within the meaning of this section.

(3.) Nothing in this Act shall affect Bills relating to the divorce or marriage of individuals, and any such Bill shall be introduced and proceed in Parliament in like manner as if this Act had not passed.

Limitation
on borrow-
ing by local
authorities.

34. The local authority for any county or borough or other area shall not borrow money without either—

(*a*) special authority from the Irish Legislature, or

(*b*) the sanction of the proper department of the Irish Government ;

and shall not, without such special authority, borrow ;

(i) in the case of a municipal borough or town or area less than a county, any loan which together with the then outstanding debt of the local authority, will exceed twice the annual rateable value of the property in the municipal borough, town, or area; or

(ii) in the case of a county or larger area, any loan which together with the then outstanding debt of the local authority, will exceed one-tenth of the annual rateable value of the property in the county or area; or

(iii) in any case a loan exceeding one-half of the above limits without a local inquiry held in the county, borough, or area by a person appointed for the purpose by the said department.

Transitory Provisions.

35.—(1.) During *three* years from the passing of this Act, and if Parliament is then sitting until the end of that session of Parliament, the Irish Legislature shall not pass an Act respecting the relations of landlord and tenant, or the sale, purchase, or letting of land generally : Provided that nothing in this section shall prevent the passing of any Irish Act with a view to the purchase of land for railways, harbours, waterworks, town improvements, or other local undertakings.

(2.) During *six* years from the passing of this Act, the appointment of a judge of the Supreme Court or other superior court in Ireland (other than one of the Exchequer judges) shall be made in pursuance of a warrant from Her Majesty countersigned as heretofore.

[margin: Temporary restriction on powers of Irish Legislature and Executive.*]*

36.—(1.) Subject to the provisions of this Act Her Majesty the Queen in Council may make or direct such arrangements as seem necessary or proper for setting in motion the Irish Legislature and Government and for otherwise bringing this Act into operation.

[margin: Transitory provisions.*]*

(2.) The Irish Legislature shall be summoned to meet on the *first Tuesday in September, one thousand eight hundred and ninety-four*, and the first election of members of the two Houses of the Irish Legislature shall be held at such time before that day, as may be fixed by Her Majesty in Council.

(3.) Upon the first meeting of the Irish Legislature the members of the House of Commons then sitting for Irish constituencies, including the members for Dublin University, shall vacate their seats, and writs shall, as soon as conveniently may be, be issued by the Lord Chancellor of Ireland for the purpose of holding an election of members to serve in Parliament for the constituencies named in the Second Schedule of this Act.

(4.) The existing Chief Baron of the Exchequer, and the senior of the existing puisne judges of the Exchequer Division of the Supreme Court, or if they or either of them are or is dead or unable or unwilling to act, such other of the judges of the Supreme Court as Her Majesty may appoint shall be the first Exchequer judges.

(5.) Where it appears to Her Majesty the Queen in Council, before the expiration of *one year* after the appointed day, that

A.D. 1893. any existing enactment respecting matters within the powers of
the Irish Legislature requires adaptation to Ireland, whether—

> (*a*) by the substitution of the Lord Lieutenant in Council, or
> of any department or officer of the executive Govern-
> ment in Ireland, for Her Majesty in Council, a Secre-
> tary of State, the Treasury, the Postmaster-General,
> the Board of Inland Revenue, or other public depart-
> ment or officer in Great Britain ; or

> (*b*) by the substitution of the Irish Consolidated Fund or
> moneys provided by the Irish Legislature for the Con-
> solidated Fund of the United Kingdom, or moneys
> provided by Parliament; or

> (*c*) by the substitution of confirmation by, or other act to be
> done by or to, the Irish Legislature for confirmation
> by or other act to be done by or to Parliament ; or

> (*d*) by any other adaptation ;

Her Majesty, by Order in Council, may make that adaptation.

(6.) Her Majesty the Queen in Council may provide for the
transfer of such property, rights, and liabilities, and the doing
of such other things as may appear to Her Majesty necessary or
proper for carrying into effect this Act or any Order in Council
under this Act.

(7.) An Order in Council under this section may make an
adaptation or provide for a transfer either unconditionally or
subject to such exceptions, conditions, and restrictions as may
seem expedient.

(8.) The draft of every Order in Council under this section
shall be laid before both Houses of Parliament for not less than
two months before it is made, and such Order when made shall,
subject as respects Ireland to the provisions of an Irish Act,
have full effect, but shall not interfere with the continued ap-
plication to any place, authority, person, or thing, not in Ireland,
of the enactment to which the Order relates.

Continu-
ance of
existing
laws, courts,
officers, &c.
37.—Except as otherwise provided by this Act, all existing
laws, institutions, authorities, and officers in Ireland, whether
judicial, administrative, or ministerial, and all existing taxes in
Ireland shall continue as if this Act had not passed, but with
the modifications necessary for adapting the same to this Act,
and subject to be repealed, abolished, altered, and adapted in
the manner and to the extent authorised by this Act.

Appointed
day.
38. Subject as in this Act mentioned the appointed day for
the purposes of this Act shall be the day of the first meeting of
the Irish Legislature, or such other day not more than *seven*
months earlier or later as may be fixed by order of Her Majesty

in Council either generally or with reference to any particular A.D. 1893.
provision of this Act, and different days may be appointed for
different purposes and different provisions of this Act, whether
contained in the same section or in different sections.

39. In this Act unless the context otherwise requires— Definitions.
The expression "existing" means existing at the passing of
this Act.

The expression "constituency" means a parliamentary constituency or a county or borough returning a member or members
to serve in either House of the Irish Legislature, as the case
requires, and the expression "parliamentary constituency"
means any county, borough, or university returning a member
or members to serve in Parliament.

The expression "parliamentary elector" means a person entitled to be registered as a voter at a parliamentary election.

The expression "parliamentary election" means the election
of a member to serve in Parliament.

The expression "tax" includes duties and fees, and the expression "duties of excise" does not include license duties.

The expression "foreign mails" means all postal packets,
whether letters, parcels, or other packets, posted in the United
Kingdom and sent to a place out of the United Kingdom, or
posted in a place out of the United Kingdom and sent to a place
in the United Kingdom, or in transit through the United
Kingdom to a place out of the United Kingdom.

The expression "telegraphic line" has the same meaning as 26 & 27 Vict.
c. 112.
in the Telegraph Acts, 1863 to 1892. 41 & 42 Vict.
c. 76.

The expression "duties on postage" includes all rates and 55 & 56 Vict.
c. 59.
sums chargeable for or in respect of postal packets, money orders, 7 Will. 4
or telegrams, or otherwise under the Post Office Acts or the and 1 Vict.
Telegraph Act, 1892. c. 36.

The expression "Irish Act" means a law made by the Irish 32 & 33 Vict.
c. 73.
Legislature. 48 & 49 Vict.
c. 58.

The expression "election laws" means the laws relating to
the election of members to serve in Parliament, other than those
relating to the qualification of electors, and includes all the
laws respecting the registration of electors, the issue and execu-
tion of writs, the creation of polling districts, the taking of the
poll, the questioning of elections, corrupt and illegal practices,
the disqualification of members and the vacating of seats.

The expression "rateable value" means the annual rateable
value under the Irish Valuation Acts.

The expression "salary" includes remuneration, allowances,
and emoluments.

The expression "pension" includes superannuation allowance.

40. This Act may be cited as the Irish Government Act, 1893. Short title.

SCHEDULES.

FIRST SCHEDULE.

LEGISLATIVE COUNCIL.

CONSTITUENCIES AND NUMBER OF COUNCILLORS.

Constituencies.	Councillors.
Antrim county	Three.
Armagh county	One.
Belfast borough	Two.
Carlow county	One.
Cavan county	One.
Clare county	One.
Cork county—	
East Riding	Three.
West Riding	One.
Cork borough	One.
Donegal county	One.
Down county	Three.
Dublin county	Three.
Dublin borough	Two.
Fermanagh county	One.
Galway county	Two.
Kerry county	One.
Kildare county	One.
Kilkenny county	One.
King's county	One.
Leitrim and Sligo counties	One.
Limerick county	Two.
Londonderry county	One.
Longford county	One.
Louth county	One.
Mayo county	One.
Meath county	One.
Monaghan county	One.
Queen's county	One.
Roscommon county	One.
Tipperary county	Two.
Tyrone county	One.
Waterford county	One.
Westmeath county	One.
Wexford county	One.
Wicklow county	One.
	Forty-eight.

The expression "borough" in this Schedule means an existing parliamentary borough.
Counties of cities and towns not named in this Schedule shall be combined with the county at large in which they are included for parliamentary elections, and if not so included, then with the county at large bearing the same name.

A borough named in this Schedule shall not for the purposes of this Schedule form part of any other constituency.

SECOND SCHEDULE.   A.D. 1893.

IRISH MEMBERS IN THE HOUSE OF COMMONS.

Constituency.	Number of Members for House of Commons.
Antrim county	Three.
Armagh county	Two.
Belfast borough (in divisions as mentioned below)	Four.
Carlow county	One.
Cavan county	Two.
Clare county	Two.
Cork county (in divisions as mentioned below)	Five.
Cork borough	Two.
Donegal county	Three.
Down county	Three.
Dublin county	Two.
Dublin borough (in divisions as mentioned below)	Four.
Fermanagh county	One.
Galway county	Three.
Galway borough	One.
Kerry county	Three.
Kildare county	One.
Kilkenny county	One.
Kilkenny borough	One.
King's county	One.
Leitrim county	Two.
Limerick county	Two.
Limerick borough	One.
Londonderry county	Two.
Londonderry borough	One.
Longford county	One.
Louth county	One.
Mayo county	Three.
Meath county	Two.
Monaghan county	Two.
Newry borough	One.
Queen's county	One.
Roscommon county	Two.
Sligo county	Two.
Tipperary county	Three.
Tyrone county	Three.
Waterford county	One.
Waterford borough	One.
Westmeath county	One.
Wexford county	Two.
Wicklow county	One.
	Eighty.

(1.) In this Schedule the expression "borough" means an existing parliamentary borough.

(2.) In the parliamentary boroughs of Belfast and Dublin, one member shall be returned by each of the existing parliamentary divisions of those boroughs, and the law relating to the divisions of boroughs shall apply accordingly.

(3.) The county of Cork shall be divided into two divisions, consisting of the East Riding and the West Riding, and three members shall be elected by the East Riding, and two members shall be elected by the West Riding; and the law relating to divisions of counties shall apply to those divisions.

THIRD SCHEDULE.

FINANCE.

IMPERIAL LIABILITIES, EXPENDITURE, AND MISCELLANEOUS REVENUE.

Liabilities.

For the purpose of this Act, "Imperial liabilities" consist of—

(1.) The funded and unfunded debt of the United Kingdom, inclusive of terminable annuities paid out of the permanent annual charge for the National Debt, and inclusive of the cost of the management of the said funded and unfunded debt, but exclusive of the Local Loans stock and Guaranteed Land stock and the cost of the management thereof; and

(2.) All other charges on the Consolidated Fund of the United Kingdom for the repayment of borrowed money, or to fulfil a guarantee.

Expenditure.

For the purpose of this Act Imperial expenditure consists of expenditure for the following services :—

I. Naval and Military expenditure (including Greenwich Hospital).

II. Civil expenditure, that is to say,—

(*a*.) Civil list and Royal Family.

(*b*.) Salaries, pensions, allowances, and incidental expenses of—

    (i.) Lord Lieutenant of Ireland ;

    (ii.) Exchequer judges in Ireland.

(*c*.) Buildings, works, salaries, pensions, printing, stationery, allowances, and incidental expenses of—

    (i.) Parliament ;

    (ii.) National Debt Commissioners ;

    (iii.) Foreign Office and diplomatic and consular service, including secret service, special services, and telegraph subsidies ;

    (iv.) Colonial Office, including special services and telegraph subsidies ;

    (v.) Privy Council ;

    (vi.) Board of Trade including the Mercantile Marine Fund, Patent Office, Railway Commission, and Wreck Commission but excluding Bankruptcy ;

    (vii.) Mint ;

    (viii.) Meteorological Society ;

    (ix.) Slave trade service.

(*d*.) Foreign mails and telegraphic communication with places outside the United Kingdom.

Revenue.

For the purposes of this Act the public revenue to a portion of which Ireland may claim to be entitled consists of revenue from the following sources :—

1. Suez Canal shares or payments on account thereof.

2. Loans and advances to foreign countries.

3. Annual payments by British possessions.

4. Fees, stamps, and extra receipts received by departments, the expenses of which are part of the Imperial expenditure.

5. Small branches of the hereditary revenues of the Crown.

6. Foreshores.

FOURTH SCHEDULE.

PROVISIONS AS TO POST OFFICE.

(1.) The Postmaster-General shall pay to the Irish Post Office in respect of any foreign mails sent through Ireland and the Irish Post Office shall pay to the Postmaster-General in respect of any foreign mails sent through Great Britain, such sum as may be agreed upon for the carriage of those mails in Ireland or Great Britain as the case may be.

(2.) The Irish Post Office shall pay to the Postmaster-General;

(i.) One half of the expense of the packet service and submarine telegraph lines between Great Britain and Ireland after deducting from that expense the sum fixed by the Postmaster-General as incurred on account of foreign mails or telegraphic communication with a place out of the United Kingdom as the case may be; and

(ii.) Five per cent of the expenses of the conveyance outside the United Kingdom of foreign mails, and of the transmission of telegrams to places outside the United Kingdom; and

(iii.) Such proportion of the receipts for telegrams to places out of the United Kingdom as is due in respect of the transmission outside the United Kingdom of such telegrams

(3.) The Postmaster-General and the Irish Post Office respectively shall pay to the other of them on account of foreign money orders, of compensation in respect of postal packets, and of any matters not specifically provided for in this Schedule such sums as may be agreed upon.

(4.) Of the existing debt incurred in respect of telegraphs, a sum of five hundred and fifty thousand pounds two and three quarters per cent Consolidated Stock shall be treated as debt of the Irish Post Office, and for paying the dividends on and redeeming such stock there shall be paid half yearly by the Irish Exchequer to the Exchequer of the United Kingdom an annuity of *eighteen* thousand pounds for *sixty* years, and such annuity when paid into the Exchequer shall be forthwith paid to the National Debt Commissioners and applied for the reduction of the National Debt.

(5.) The Postmaster-General and the Irish Post Office may agree on the facilities to be afforded by the Irish Post Office in Ireland in relation to any matters the administration of which by virtue of this Act remains with the Postmaster-General, and with respect to the use of the Irish telegraphic lines for through lines in connection with submarine telegraphs, or with telegraphic communication with any place out of the United Kingdom.

FIFTH SCHEDULE.

REGULATIONS AS TO GRATUITIES AND PENSIONS FOR CIVIL SERVANTS.

SIXTH SCHEDULE.

PART I.

REGULATIONS AS TO ESTABLISHMENT OF POLICE FORCES AND AS TO THE
ROYAL IRISH CONSTABULARY AND DUBLIN METROPOLITAN POLICE
CEASING TO EXIST.

(1.) Such local police forces shall be established under such local
authorities and for such counties, municipal boroughs, or other larger areas,
as may be provided by Irish Act.

(2.) Whenever the Executive Committee of the Privy Council in Ireland
certify to the Lord Lieutenant that a police force adequate for local
purposes, has been established in any area, then, subject to the provisions of
this Act, he shall within six months thereafter direct the Royal Irish
Constabulary to be withdrawn from the performance of regular police duties
in such area, and such order shall be forthwith carried into effect.

(3.) Upon any such withdrawal the Lord Lieutenant shall order measures
to be taken for a proportionate reduction of the numbers of the Royal Irish
Constabulary, and such order shall be duly executed.

(4.) Upon the Executive Committee of the Privy Council in Ireland
certifying to the Lord Lieutenant that adequate local police forces have been
established in every part of Ireland, then, subject to the provisions of this
Act, the Lord Lieutenant shall within six months after such certificate,
order measures to be taken for causing the whole of the Royal Irish Constabulary to cease to exist as a police force, and such order shall be duly
executed.

(5.) Where the area in which a local police force is established is part of
the Dublin Metropolitan Police District, the foregoing regulations shall apply
to the Dublin Metropolitan Police in like manner as if that force were the
Royal Irish Constabulary.

PART II.

REGULATIONS AS TO GRATUITIES AND PENSIONS FOR THE ROYAL IRISH
CONSTABULARY AND DUBLIN METROPOLITAN POLICE.

SEVENTH SCHEDULE.

REGULATIONS AS TO HOUSES OF THE LEGISLATURE AND THE
MEMBERS THEREOF.

Legislative Council.

(1.) There shall be a separate register of electors of councillors of the
Legislative Council which shall be made, until otherwise provided by Irish
Act, in like manner as the parliamentary register of electors.

(2.) Where, for the election of councillors any counties are combined so as to form one constituency, then until otherwise provided by Irish Act,

(*a*) the returning officer for the whole constituency shall be that one of the returning officers for Parliamentary elections for those counties to whom the writ is addressed, and the writ shall be addressed to the returning officer for the constituency with the largest population, according to the census of 1891.

(*b*) the returning officer shall have the same authority throughout the whole constituency as a returning officer at a Parliamentary election for a county has in the county.

(*c*) the registers of electors of each county shall jointly be the register of electors for the constituency.

(*d*) for the purposes of this Schedule "county" includes a county of a city or town, and this Schedule, and the law relating to the qualification of electors shall apply, as if the county of a city or town formed part of the county at large with which it is combined, and the qualification in the county of a city or town shall be the same as in such county at large.

(3.) Writs shall be issued for the election of councillors at such time not less than one nor more than three months before the day for the periodical retirement of councillors as the Lord Lieutenant in Council may fix.

(4.) The day for the periodical retirement of councillors shall until otherwise provided by Irish Act be the last day of August in every fourth year.

(5.) For the purposes of such retirement, the constituencies shall be divided into two equal divisions, and the constituencies in each province shall be divided as nearly as may be equally between those divisions, and constituencies returning two or more members shall be treated as two or more constituencies, and placed in both divisions.

(6.) Subject as aforesaid, the particular constituencies which are to be in each division shall be determined by lot.

(7.) The said division and lot shall be made and conducted before the appointed day in manner directed by the Lord Lieutenant in Council.

(8.) The first councillors elected for the constituencies in the first division shall retire on the first day of retirement which occurs after the first meeting of the Irish Legislature, and the first councillors for the constituencies in the second division shall retire on the second day of retirement after that meeting.

(9.) Any casual vacancy among the councillors shall be filled by a new election, but the councillor filling the vacancy shall retire at the time at which the vacating councillor would have retired.

Legislative Assembly.

(10.) The Parliamentary register of electors for the time being shall, until otherwise provided by Irish Act, be the register of electors of the Legislative Assembly.

Both Houses.

(11.) Until otherwise provided by Irish Act, the Lord Lieutenant in Council may make regulations for adapting the existing election laws to the election of members of the two Houses of the Legislature.

(12.) Annual sessions of the Legislature shall be held.

(13.) Any peer, whether of the United Kingdom, Great Britain, England, Scotland, or Ireland shall be qualified to be a member of either House.

(14.) A member of either House may by writing under his hand resign his seat, and the same shall thereupon be vacant.

(15.) The same person shall not be a member of both Houses.

A.D. 1893.   (16.) Until otherwise provided by Irish Act, if the same person is elected
to a seat in each House, he shall, before the eighth day after the next sitting
of either House, by written notice, elect in which House he will serve, and
upon such election his seat in the other House shall be vacant, and if he
does not so elect, his seat in both Houses shall be vacant.

(17.) Until otherwise provided by Irish Act, any such notice electing in
which House a person will sit, or any notice of resignation, shall be given
in manner directed by the Standing Orders of the Houses, and if there is no
such direction, shall be given to the Lord Lieutenant.

(18.) The powers of either House shall not be affected by any vacancy
therein, or any defect in the election or qualification of any member thereof.

(19.) Until otherwise provided by Irish Act the holders of such Irish
offices as may be named by Order of the Queen in Council before the
appointed day, shall be entitled to be elected to and sit in either House
notwithstanding that they hold offices under the Crown, but on acceptance
of any such office the seat of any such person in either House shall be
vacated unless he has accepted the office in succession to some other of the
said offices.

(20.) The Lord Lieutenant in Council may, before the appointed day
make regulations for the following purposes:—

(*a.*) The making of a register of electors of councillors in time for the
election of the first councillors, and with that object for the varia-
tion of the days relating to registration in the existing election
laws, and for prescribing the duties of officers, and for making
such adaptations of those laws as appear necessary or proper for
duly making a register ;

(*b.*) The summoning of the two Houses of the Legislature of Ireland, the
issue of writs and any other things appearing to be necessary or
proper for the election of members of the two Houses ;

(*c.*) The election of a chairman (whether called Speaker, President, or by
any other name,) of each House, the quorum of each House, the
communications between the two Houses, and such adaptation to
the proceedings of the two Houses of the procedure of Parliament,
as appears expedient for facilitating the conduct of business by
those Houses on their first meeting ;

(*d.*) The adaptation to the two Houses and the members thereof of any
laws and customs relating to the House of Commons or the
members thereof ;

(*e.*) The deliberation and voting together of the two Houses in cases
provided by this Act.

(21.) The regulations may be altered by Irish Act, and also in so far as
they concern the procedure of either House alone, by Standing Orders of
that House, but shall, until altered, have effect as if enacted in this Act.

Printed by PONSONBY AND WELDRICK, *Dublin.*

www.ingramcontent.com/pod-product-compliance
Lightning Source LLC
Chambersburg PA
CBHW021627270326
41931CB00008B/905